Day Trading:

10 Best Beginners Strategies to Start Trading Like A Pro and Control Your Emotions in Stock, Penny Stock, Real Estate, Options Trading, Forex, Cryptocurrencies, Futures, Swing Trading

The following eBook is reproduced below with the goal of providing information that is as accurate and reliable as possible. Regardless, purchasing this eBook can be seen as consent to the fact that both the publisher and the author of this book are in no way experts on the topics discussed within and that any recommendations or suggestions that are made herein are for entertainment purposes only. Professionals should be consulted as needed prior to undertaking any of the action endorsed herein.

This declaration is deemed fair and valid by both the American Bar Association and the Committee of Publishers Association and is legally binding throughout the United States.

Furthermore, the transmission, duplication, or reproduction of any of the following work including specific information will be considered an illegal act irrespective of if it is done electronically or in print. This extends to creating a secondary or tertiary copy of the work or a recorded copy and is only allowed with an expressed written consent from the Publisher. All additional rights reserved.

The information in the following pages is broadly considered to be a truthful and accurate account of facts and as such any inattention, use, or misuse of the information in question by the reader will render any resulting actions solely under their purview. There are no scenarios in which the publisher or the original author of this work can be in any fashion deemed liable for any hardship or damages that may befall them after undertaking information described herein.

Additionally, the information in the following pages is intended only for informational purposes and should thus be thought of as universal. As befitting its nature, it is presented without assurance regarding its prolonged validity or interim quality. Trademarks that are mentioned are done without written consent and can in no way be considered an endorsement from the trademark holder.

Table of Contents

Introduction

Congratulations on downloading your personal copy of *Day Trading* and thank you for doing so.

In this guidebook, we are going to spend some time learning about stocks and why they are one of the best options to consider when it is time to get into the world of trading. While there are many options that come from working inside the world of trading, stocks can be an interesting choice that will bring in a lot of profit. This guidebook is going to go over them in more detail so that you can learn how to use this investing tool.

First, we will start with some of the basics of stocks and how they are different from the other assets that you can choose from and we will discuss the two main options with stocks namely the Pink Sheets and the Over-the-Counter Bulletins. Once we have had a chance for you to learn about these basics, it is time to get into the world of stock investing. We will talk about how to get into the game and find a good broker before moving into some of the top strategies that you can use to put your money to work and see the stocks work for you. We will then end the guidebook with some basic tips that can help you to really improve your results even as an advanced investor.

Working with stocks is a great way to open up your portfolio so that your money can grow more than ever before, but it does take some time and effort in order to learn this method and get it to work well for you. This guidebook is going to give you the tips that you need in order to get started making a good income with stocks.

There are plenty of books on this subject on the market. Thanks again for choosing this one! Every effort was made to ensure it is full of as much useful information as possible. Please enjoy!

Chapter 1: Trading Stocks

Investing today seems like a really difficult undertaking. The crisis of Western economies and finances makes any prediction risky, so much so that we can say that the last decade has shown that.

Finance is the science of hindsight.

Every thud has always been explained with this or that and with a great deal of detail. Interesting investments have always been justified by reading the data of the past in a certain way, so that finance has become easy prey to the effect result: anyone who had guessed an investment flaunted the four winds while those who had lost it shut up for not making the figure of the chicken; the first became the new guru, except to be denied to the first debacle.

In order to become successful financially and in stock investing, it is extremely important to have a deep knowledge of what the stock market is and how money actually works. In order to do this, one cannot avoid a deep study of personal finance and of the big economy machine that we all live into. By opening your mind on what money truly is (exchange of value), you will be able to change your mind set about it and start taking different actions that will lead to your success. We hope that by reading this book, you will grasp the necessary nuggets for you to make a positive change in your life, as everyone can reach financial abundance.

Investing is not for everyone

If you have small amounts of money, it is simplistic to hope to speculate on it and to earn something that turns it into a treasure; first of all, there is the risk that a sudden event (the classic marriage of a child, a large unexpected expense, etc.) forces to disinvest at the very moment when it is not convenient to do so, with serious losses.

Secondly, investing small sums does not allow management expenses to be managed well, and even any earnings do not change their lives (1% of 10,000 Euros are 100 Euros). Therefore, only those sums of which long-term availability and a minimum of 50,000 Euros are to be reserved for complex investments.

If the two conditions for investing (stability and quantity of capital) are not met, it is appropriate to divert their savings towards highly liquid forms of investment (for example, online current account, short-term government bonds, etc.) with the only one aim to lose as little as possible with respect to inflation (look at these points in more detail in our article Investment Strategies).

If the two conditions are satisfied, let's start by saying that there are two ways to operate:

Getting advice from a consultant

With the term consultant, we do not mean a physical person as much as the source of information: it can be the financial promoter, a banker, the "expert" friend, but also the business newspaper, the Internet site, etc.

The first way to operate has led many to rather mediocre results. If world-class economists cannot predict anything for sure, it is optimistic to hope that an "amateur" can do better.

Suppose you have a capital of 100,000 Euros and you are so good that you get 3% above inflation: it means 3,000 Euros. If this involves dedicating one hour a day to follow the markets, it is equivalent to a net salary of 24,000 Euros per year (1 hour per day = 3,000 Euros of income equivalent to an 8-hour job giving 8 × 3,000 = 24,000 Euros that is, my work in finance makes me like a job that gives € 24,000 a year), not much!

The second way minimizes the costs of management time, but it is advisable that the consultant is trusted and proposes tools that the client understands "to understand" (for example, if you do not know what covered warrants are, it is insane to invest in them just because someone recommended them); it is, therefore, necessary that, even in the case of the consultant, there is a minimum acculturation on the instruments.

It is necessary to take into account that, often, there is a personal interest in those who advise (for example, the financial promoter who advises bonds of their bank) and this can undermine the goodness of the board.

More often than not, it is unwise to rely on the authoritativeness of the consultant because, let us remember, authoritativeness does not mean reliability. So, we try to know the professionalism and honesty of those who propose, starting from the assumption that in these times, those who propose speculative investments only to satisfy the customer's desire for profit is neither honest nor professional.

The term speculation has, in the common language, a rather negative value. Speculation is usually a form of investment in which the forecasting activity is purely subjective: the investor has certain expectations that, if realized, generate a profit, otherwise, a loss.

From a psychological point of view, speculation can be of two types: active or passive. Active speculation occurs when the subject with previous actions, desired (often with the aid of not entirely legal means) or fortuitous, has a degree of information superior to a generic participant of the market in which he operates. It is passive when a surplus of information is lacking, and the investment is made on the basis of general considerations.

A case of active speculation occurs when X buys agricultural land, knowing that he will be under construction and that it will soon become a building; instead, it is passive the action of Y who acquires a land hoping that, sooner or later, it will become a building. The action of Y can turn into a boomerang when his land is expropriated, perhaps at a slightly lower price

8

than the purchase price, for the construction of a road!

Another example of passive speculation is, for example, in the technological field when Z decides to buy the shares of a multinational company because "we know" that this will put on the market a fantastic computer. Since everyone knows it, it is unthinkable that such trivial news can generate profit. It often happens that the stock goes up and then collapses to the first difficulties of the new product before Z has time to sell his shares. Even in this case, only the active speculator, who "before" others know what will happen, will be able to make profits.

Generally, it is optimistic to hope to earn with passive speculations.

People keep trying because the rumours of successful speculation spread and the voices of bankruptcy "die". The speech is very similar to that of non-fair games: passive speculation is a lot of those who like to believe that economics is a science with easily predictable results. If that were the case, the major economists would be the richest men on Earth, which is not (not by chance a well-known statement speaks of the economy as the less exact science after ... astrology).

Sometimes, passive speculation also manifests itself as a simple idea (which anyone could have) that is not critically tested but is optimistically accepted. The idea itself could be good, but what makes it doubtful is the lack of analysis.

Let's see an example. I decide to buy a house with a mortgage, to rent it, to pay the mortgage with the rent, and to find myself after 25 years owner of a house without having paid a euro. The idea looks good and I'll throw myself. A more cautious person would have at least implemented analysis of the problem to see the possible advantages of the operation (without falling in love with his idea).

Here is a very simplified analysis.

For reasons of simplicity, suppose that in the 25 years, inflation is nothing (if it were not, should we consider returns, we must consider them net of inflation). It is indeed important to understand the role of any inflation in the model.

1. Property value: 140,000.
2. A loan of 140,000 Euros (25 years): 900 monthly approximately
3. Unfurnished local rent: 4% of the value.
4. Initial costs: € 18,000; the initial costs are 10% of taxes for the second home (as a builder), notary fees, the ignition of the mortgage.
5. Extraordinary expenses: 7,000 Euros over 25 years; they are mainly the expenses for the purchase of the boilers (average life 8-10 years) and the painting of the rooms. They are 350 Euros a year or so.
6. Ordinary expenses: 1,000 Euros per year (taxes, boiler maintenance, insurance, etc.).
7. Personal management expenses: 1,000 Euros (50 hours x 20 Euros per hour); they must be counted even if the management is done directly by the owner.
8. The annual total of expenses (extraordinary, ordinary, and management) is € 2,350.

It is supposed not to furnish the premises because this, in the face of an increase in rent (let's say a possible 5%), would entail the need to purchase and renovate furniture for the tenants over the next 25 years.

Every year, 10,500 Euros are spent on the loan and 5,600 are collected. Since we pay taxes (we assume a rate of about 30%) on 85% of the rent, there will be about 4,200 Euros net.

In total, we will have to pay about € 8,950 a year, that is, over € 225,000 to be added to the initial costs of € 18,000.

In 25 years, we will, therefore, pay a figure well above the value of the property: due to the mortgage, we will be under about 100,000 Euros compared to the original value of the property. If the house will actually be re-evaluated (i.e. net of inflation) of this sum, we will break even. Most likely, the securities market will also be re-evaluated, and we would still have to compare the result with what we would have invested every year for the sums paid for the house.

From this data, it seems to be certainly cheaper and less engaging to simply invest the approximately 9,000 Euros of expenses per year.

If you were to fall in love with your idea and want to "get it back at any cost," you would have to investigate the following possibilities:

1. Can I get a lot more than 4% rent?
2. Should I furnish the apartment for a little more rent?
3. Can I get a more favourable mortgage?
4. Can I minimize initial, management, ordinary, and extraordinary expenses?

Obviously, I can also pose more general problems:

1. What "economic" problems can I have from tenants?
2. Will not I be discovered for some time?
3. How much can the house be re-evaluated after inflation?
4. How much could my money be re-evaluated (always net of inflation) if I decide to make an accumulation plan to buy the house after 25 years? Etc.

As you can see, it is not possible to make a sensible decision without exact and very detailed data. This is the fundamental difference between passive speculation and a prudent investment.

Chapter 2: Trading a Large Capital

This question would require a whole book to be eviscerated (and maybe I will write one about it in the next future), so it is more appropriate to warn you of the big mistakes that suggest fine operational details.

First of all, without real competence, it is quite absurd to throw yourself in too complicated things (for example, high-risk long-term actions). Of course, you can get help from an expert, but then you can totally trust him. In this case, it is useful to understand that, if not even a Nobel Prize for the economy can foresee profitable investments, how much more a simple banking?

In economics, too many people sell expertise by exploiting favourable moments, except when the favourable moments are not to blame the astral conjunctures.

There is a famous saying that *economics is the second less reliable science, second only to astrology.*

In the real estate market, it is optimistic to hope to buy one or more houses and earn money automatically. It also takes a certain competence of the affair, a certain vision of the future (that is, of what is re-valued and what does not, maybe because, after ten years, you build a landfill nearby) or (rents) you need to calculate the time from devotee to the management of the property, taxes, etc.

In the securities market, it's even worse because so many beautiful tools delude you to make money.

The point is that who sells you a product is based on what happened in the past, without saying clearly that the past with the future has little to do with it (also because a few decades are not statistically significant to deduce something sensible). Not surprisingly, I do not know if you know, but in recent years, it was really for a few to have a net gain (i.e. removed inflation and management fees), many have simply lost.

Individual risks must also be mentioned: too many people invest a sum believing that they can withdraw at any moment (I marry, I have to buy the new house, the new car, I have to give a present to my son, etc.). Disaster. The "moment" always comes when your investments go down. The more one looks for a probable gain, the more he exposes himself to risks. Admitted and not granted that one can earn 2% net per year (i.e. over 20% in 10 years), in the ten years, there may be a period of 2-3 years in which you are under 5%. If the "moment" of sales arrives in that period, it would be worth investing in a "smart" strategy. So, you can invest a lot, knowing that for 10 years, you do not touch it and that you can touch it only if you are active. If you need substantial liquidity, you should not invest in medium to long-term choices.

Currently, if a person has a serious capital (i.e. that can leave still for a medium-long time) of less than 100,000 Euros, it is better to invest only in safe and very short-term products, content with not losing on inflation. If capital is higher, it is convenient or to become experts (but not those who delude themselves to break everything because funds, bonds, and shares risk becoming the lottery of those who are only slightly more intelligent than others) or rely on a competent person, realistic and honest. To skim the aspirants, try to ask what net gain a person can expect with x euro (shoot high): if they answer with "definitely at least y%" and y exceeds a few percentage points, forget it.
I wondered only if a person could have other income, in addition to those due to work.

I do not think anyone can refute this statement: *there is no one (Nobel Prize or society) that can guarantee a decent profit (that is deductible expenses and inflation), that is some percentage points.*

Let's deviate for a second from the stock market in order to see another market with huge potential for those who have big sums of money to invest. We are talking about the real estate market, which nowadays is becoming more and more popular. Now, this is not a book about real estate or property trading, but we still wanted to give you some piece of advice to take your hard-earned trading profits and invest them in a longer-term market.

The activity of a real estate investor is often misunderstood. Most people, when they hear the term "real estate investor" think "okay, who does this job earns a lot of money, it is fun, it is easy to do, and it is all sunshine and rainbows", but the reality is not like that. At all. This information that is disseminated all around the internet is not correct. The activity carried out by a real estate investor is a methodical activity; it is an activity that takes a long time to master. The investors have to do a lot of visits to real estates, he has to make a lot of proposals knowing that most of these offers will be rejected, as you can imagine.

It is important to operate with a large number of real estate visits and proposals to obtain results. In other words, the idea that the real estate investor walks and makes money is absolutely false; it is a very difficult job.

What I would like to tell you is that this is an extraordinary profession, where you can obtain very important personal and economic satisfaction, but it is necessary to work hard. It is necessary to have a lot of time and it is necessary to know from the beginning that it will not be easy. If you could automatically earn, everybody would do it, which is absolutely not real, we know it very well. To do something and get a result, you need to commit, so if you are interested in the world of real estate investments, you must know that it is a difficult job like all other investments. It is a job where you'll have to spend time, where most of the answers you receive will be no, you will not have to give up, you'll have to continue and if you manage to be consistent and do things the right way, you will be able to clearly get results not only at the economic level but also at the level of personal satisfaction.

Before getting started with the 15 Golden lessons of real estate investing, it is important to make a quick note about mindset.

Your dream house is not an investment, did you know that?

The property owned, or the house of our dreams - or villa, has always been considered a sacred "asset" in America. A goal to be achieved as soon as possible at the cost of any sacrifice. And indeed, we are the people with the highest percentage of homeowners. About 80% of Americans own a home. It does not matter if we take out mortgages for thirty years (sometimes even longer) with monstrous instalments that most often absorb around 50% of the income of an average family. The important thing is to "own" our home. Good, this is what smart people do, right? False. Almost nobody that is rich lives in a place he owns. As Grant Cardone says, "rent where you live and own what you can rent".

The question I want to ask you now is this: do you think buying a house is equivalent to buying an asset or a liability? The answer is clear and not debatable. Among the mortgage payment, various charges, government, and municipal taxes, when buying a house, you buy a liability.

But we better explain the concept of liability. By liability we mean, everything that generates cash outflow from our family income statement. By contrast, by asset, we mean everything that generates positive cash flow. Example, I buy an obligation that usually brings a coupon. This coupon represents an income, and therefore, the obligation is an asset.

The sad truth of the American real estate market

But how strange: we make so many sacrifices to buy a house, yet we buy a liability? Yes, dear readers, in America, unfortunately, the investment property is almost completely unknown. In fact, there is no real estate market in the true sense of the word. And for the real estate market, I mean the sale of an asset, in this case, the house, in order to realize a capital gain, and therefore, an investment income. Trades usually in America in the vast majority of cases are made because a couple decides to get married and then buy a house, or move after the coming of children, etc. In summary, it is more like following a family necessity and not for making an investment, as what usually happens for financial or business investments.

The ventures of real estate investing

But at this point, the question to be asked is this: is it possible to transform the purchase of a house from a liability into an asset and consequently obtain a monthly income or make a capital gain? Well, dear readers, the answer is fortunately yes! Not only is it possible, but it is desirable that each of us in the investment process of their assets dedicate part of the capital to real estate investments.

Real estate investing has some notable advantages, for example, it is possible to receive monthly income (rents) and at the same time realize capital gains at the time of sale. Precisely because of the characteristics of the market in consideration, such as the American one, the investment in real estate, in fact, is a more than secure investment, as the "home" good in America will hardly lose value.

The recent crisis has confirmed this theory. Practically in the whole world, the real estate market has undergone very heavy devaluations even in the order of 50-60%, not only in America but also in Spain, England, etc. In America, there was only a stagnation of prices and a lengthening of the time of purchase. But, in fact, the market has not fallen below 5% (obviously should be made distinctions according to regions, city type of properties, central or peripheral, etc ...)

Now, it is time to take a look at 5 advanced rules to keep in mind when investing in the real estate market.

Invest in houses that you will rent

We hypothesize to buy a house of $200,000 with a minimum investment of $40,000 (but there are banks that also finance 100% of the amount), and that with the rent, we cover only the mortgage payment. Well, after 10 years assuming an average revaluation of 4%, our house has been re-valued for a value of $296,000 c.a which means that $40,000 has become 96,000 in 10 years. In practice, an annual profit of 14%. Not bad, I would say, if compared to the yields of bonds and some liquidity/money funds that fill the wallets of American savers. In reality, the above calculations are not complete. As they do not consider the purchase and sale charges (taxes, notary, etc.) and the additional capital gain. In fact, paying the instalment of the silent, the tenant also pays us a portion of the capital loaned by the bank; which means that when we sell, in addition to the revaluation of $96,000, we will have to add the missing principal amount to be returned to the bank net of transaction costs.

From liability to an asset

We hypothesize that we managed to buy a good deal and that therefore the property, net of the mortgage, and the charges, generates a small monthly income deriving from the rent. Suddenly, what was a liability becomes a monthly income, even if only a few hundred dollars, it is an addition to your income.

Buy only amazing deals, especially at the beginning

In order for the rent to exceed the instalments of the silent, it is necessary to buy well. Buying a good deal means essentially at a good price. Opportunities are there, they simply have to be found. Some small suggestions are:

1. Avoid the agencies
2. Find private vendors
3. Walk around the neighbourhoods that interest you to look for property for sale

4. Talk to the doorkeepers
5. Attend the Auctions in court. Only this aspect should be explored with an ad hoc article.
   For the moment, it is enough to know that the system has become absolutely transparent and secure. So, you just have to find the right opportunity. You can buy houses even with 30/40% discount on the real value
6. Read the announcements and identify the "needy" people to sell
7. Buy in central and/or valuable areas. It is the only guarantee for not having a bad surprise

Apply leverage on your money

Fundamental. We have seen that buying a house with an initial investment could even generate a monthly income. Well, let's imagine replicating the investment with the same characteristics at least 3 times and we hypothesize to be able to get 300/month from each of our rents (net of charges and taxes). In fact, with $900/month of capital gain, we are able to safely pay a good instalment of a mortgage for the purchase of another house, and here comes the nice one, paid entirely with the revenue from the rents. I leave to you the imagination of how many times it is possible to replicate the above investment scheme and calculate the benefits. It is just amazing.

Only take mortgages with fix interest rates

When you engage in real estate investing, you are already taking a "business" risk; you do not need to take other risks such as interest rate related risk. Let me explain better when buying an investment property, I need to know exactly how much is the monthly exit (instalment + charges) in order to correctly calculate the expected cash flow. Only careful planning of income and expenses can lead to a correct real estate investment. The accuracy of the calculations can make the difference between a successful and a non-profitable investment.

And finally, let's see 10 other tips to invest a big heritage in the real estate market.

1. Understand the peculiarity of the real estate market

The "brick", as the real estate market was called fifty years ago, is a market like any other. Remember: in finance, there is never a 100% safe investment! Each market has its own peculiarities, has its ups and downs, and even the real estate market is a market that does not escape these logics. Investing in bricks can be useful and can offer interesting perspectives, but it is good that you first inform yourself before taking this step.

Do not limit yourself to looking at stock prices, but if you plan to buy an apartment or a box or another property, take a trip around the area. Consult the prices displayed outside the various real estate agencies in the district and compare them. Often, even within the same city, prices change significantly from district to district. This happens because the costs of a real estate property are closely linked to the area in which it is built: if it is in the suburbs, it will cost less than an exactly identical property but located in the city centre.
Furthermore, prices are also dependent on so-called connected services. For example, a three-room apartment has a certain cost if it is located in a condominium where there is a garden with its green care service by a specialized company, or there is a concierge service; an apartment with the exact same size but placed in a condominium without a green care service or porter will have a lower price.

2. Learn what is best to buy and what to stay away from

The very first choice that can be made, in terms of buying real estate as an investment, is certainly buying a small apartment - a studio or a two-room apartment - that is located in a central area, well served by public transport, and that has at least one connected parking space, if not a garage. This would be the best solution. Why?

A small apartment is much easier to rent than a large one. Leasing an apartment to a family is very risky: you can go to cases of insolvency, and if there are children in the family, submitting an injunction to eviction not only can be very complicated but you may not even be able to free your apartment. And so, you would find yourself in the unpleasant situation of not being able to dispose of your personal assets and having to deal with insolvent tenants: they are two big problems, as you can imagine.

Instead, a studio or a two-room apartment can be rented to a professional who has moved to the city for work reasons. A person who does not have a dependent family but has a solid salary behind him is a guarantee of solvency and also, if the apartment you need or decide that it is time to resell it, you would have no difficulty in freeing it within the established time frame. If the studio can also combine a parking space - even if, we repeat, the box is the best solution - the added value of your property grows, especially if it is located in an area where parking can be a problem: with a more value added, you can ask for a slightly larger rent. But you should still be careful not to propose a fee outside of the logic of the market! You would risk never having a tenant, and then you would not even have an income.

Finally, consideration on the location of the studio: central area and served by public transport. The central area because, usually, the city centres are lively areas, with rich proposals for both day and nightlife; but it is essential that there is also an excellent public transport service in the proximity of your apartment so that future tenants, if they do not want to use the car for movements, would still have the opportunity to go anywhere.

3. Studying other real estate opportunities

The box is a very interesting alternative to a standard one room apartment. First of all, the costs of a box are much, much smaller than those of an apartment, and this is definitely an advantage. Even if there were extraordinary condo fees in the complex where your garage is located, the rates for you would be very low because it is proportionate to the small number of thousandths of which you are the owner. Moreover, when buying a box, you should not worry about expenses related to the makeover and upholding of the domestic systems nor should you worry about restructuring or upgrading costs of sorts.

And then, if you make the smart choice to buy a box in an area where there is a lot of parking, you may have a very high probability of renting it. And not only that, you could find tenants very quickly; the replacement would be guaranteed in a very short time. Last but not the least, the purchase of a box provides for a lower initial expenditure than that of an apartment: this means that, by renting it, you would be more quickly covered in expenses incurred.

4. Always look for the right deal and not the right property

Many investors in real estate investments are influenced by their feelings. A property is not money. You can see it, touch it, you can like it or not, and all this affects our taste, our feelings precisely, which can compromise what our brain would say instead. To be able to be objective, we must detach from the building and we must focus on our real goal, the deal. We must estrange from the property itself and look at all the economic aspects (cost, estimated costs of maintenance, condominium costs, classification value, and cadastral income that affect taxes, commercial compatibility of the property, and the area in which it is located in its market). It is clear that a beautiful property in a beautiful area can affect our senses more than a sad apartment in a suburban area, but often, properties in suburban residential areas can be obtained at low costs, excellent profits, and continuity. Sometimes, we strive to be objective, but when we fall in love with something, that objectivity fails without us even realizing it. It is at this moment that the role of our real estate consultant (that brings us back to the reality of the business, making us awaken from that 'falling in love) can be decisively preventing us from making a mistake that could cost us a bad deal.

5. The income from a building must be seen in the continuity of the long term

Sometimes, when assessing the profitability of a property, you look only at the maximum peak that the property can make without taking into account the time needed to make that property profitable.

Let's take a classic example, small property in a highly residential area of high value. Clearly, it is a building that can produce a high return and many dwell only on this without taking into account the fact that it is a property that can be used for short periods giving long breaks in which the income becomes a cost (tax, condominium). It is necessary time or costs (of real estate agencies) to get that income and can also be incurred more often than the maintenance costs, in addition to risking more easily the problematic situations or arrears that, although kept under control with the right tools, lead at least to an increase of time to devote to the problem (if not incurred expenses or lost revenue).

6. The real estate deal is made at the time of purchase and not of sale

Those who can buy with a substantial discount will never make mistakes. It may not be the most easily marketable building on the market, but when you have a substantial margin to sell it, everything becomes much simpler, safer, and more profitable.

On the contrary, those who buy without getting a good discounted deal, that is at market price, counting on the fact that the market will rise, can easily find themselves in an uncomfortable position, given that even in a situation like the current one where prices are low and is actually the time to buy to do business, certainties about a further downturn or a safe short-term recovery do not exist, while those who buy below cost have the certainty of being able to resell at least the market price that would allow them to make a profit (if the market goes up, it can become an exceptional profit).

But at this point, the question is *how do you buy at a discounted price?* The answer is simple. You must look (and the market is always full of them, but especially in times of crisis like these) for a motivated seller, or someone who wants to sell, who no longer wants to keep that property for any given reason. It is useless to waste time with someone who has obviously time or money and wants to make the maximum profit. On the other hand, you should always look for someone who does not have time and maybe even money. It will certainly be a motivated seller and ready to buy your real estate deal with a substantial discount.

7. Learn how to set up and conduct a negotiation

There are various factors ranging from experience and skills in the industry: from personal attitude (it's a bit like the good poker player who must have innate qualities to be able to bluff and bring his opponent straight to the goal that has been set, and other qualities that will instead refine with time and experience) to coldness and impartiality with respect to the affair.

It is clear that a good consultant will have all these characteristics of an expert who knows the techniques to be used in a negotiation, for example, a simple but always effective rule to follow is to never say a price first. It is statistically proven that the first to make a price by discovering, even if partially, their cards will eventually have a good chance of making the worst deal. The same building may be worth very different prices that depend fundamentally on the specific negotiating position of the parties and the respective ability to know how to conduct a negotiation. But a good consultant will also have the enormous advantage over the counterpart (and the investor represented) to be a third party, cold compared to the property and the deal, ready to lose the property and even the deal (if the deal is no longer detecting oneself) without those guilt and loss of senses that strike those who are about to reach the coveted object and suddenly see it slip out of hand (a certain element that often leads one of the parties when in negotiation to personally give up at a point or memento that will cost him inexorably a large part or all of his own profit), without considering that the third party consultant will have more chances to influence the counterpart towards his own objective of the part that will always be seen as an antagonist.

8. Being able to buy without or with very little money and zero risk

The most substantial real estate profit is always without costs. With huge advantages compared to investing with money. So always buy with as little money as possible, or even better, without your own money.

Do you have a bank fund? Of course it is possible, but unless you are in relationships or positions such that the lenders offer you easy money at very low costs or conditions, which happens in very few cases for very few categories of investors, the Banks, for costs and conditions imposed, are the worst way to get the necessary money for your investment.

The solution is to charge your real estate investment to three different parties, either alternatively or cumulatively. The first is a subject interested in living in the building. A formula that is increasingly successful is the rent with redemption, a form of atypical contract (which with the use is being typed) that mixes lease and sale. Imagine to finding a seller who, in order to get rid of the property, is willing to rent it with a redemption. We could propose a similar formula but more advantageous (fiscally) to this seller. We imagine proposing a preliminary contract with a payment in installments (at three years if we want more transcription if we are not interested in transcribing), the seller accepts (becoming our second investor) attracted by the possibility of getting rid of the property (or at least to forfeit the deposit after three years), and above all, to get rid of expenses and of the real estate taxation that belongs to the owner. We, investors, do not spend a dollar. We limit ourselves to finding a tenant (the one who pays our real estate investment) that occupies the property. You deliver the money to be transferred to the owner in instalment as a deposit (as well as advance on the price), and at the end of the three years (or longer period agreed), we will have (without having spent a single dollar) the possibility of buying a property whose price has already been partially paid with that deposit actually paid by the tenant, now being able to evaluate, if in the past years in the market, it climbed and the property has been appreciated or not. We will have 3 possibilities that are abstractly verifiable:

1. The market has grown, and the property has appreciated. We hypothesize a property for which, at the time, was agreed on the price of 500 thousand dollars of which 50 thousand was already paid in the form of instalment. We imagine that the property is worth 600 thousand today. We can pay it 450 thousand (or we can offer the purchase, if we do not have money available to a financing partner, third party that could finance our real estate investment, which paying it in full or in part based on its real value of 600 thousand allows us to conclude an excellent profit, with certainty

and without risking our money at the end and minimally).

2. The market has remained stable, so in our example, the property is still worth 500 thousand, but we will pay 450 thousand, being a part already paid by our tenant. In this case, however, we will have made a good profit, although not as exceptional as in the previous case.

3. The market has dropped a lot. It is the worst-case scenario in which if we had invested our money, we would have made a substantial loss or we should keep the property locked for years waiting for better times. But with our strategy, we can decide not to buy the property without losing anything. The deposit will be paid by our tenant and we were able to exit at no cost from the worst situation that could happen, virtually eliminating risks and losses.

The exemplified use of the preliminary contract and the deposit is only one of the many examples that explain how the knowledge of contracts and real estate tax that every real good real estate consultant should know that can bring a lot of value to the new investor.

9. Learn how to save money on the investment

At a time like this when the tax oppression has reached a very high level in all sectors (and especially in the real estate industry), the result of any investment can never reach (except in exceptional cases) the return that can be guaranteed by significant tax savings. So, if the real estate profit that I can go to realize can also be halved by the weight of the tax, it is clear that, if I find the way to avoid that tax oppression (or at least reduce it enormously), I can have a higher profit. So, the golden rule is to find the way to adopt those contractual-tax measures (and there are really dozens of atypical contracts usable in this regard) that can, through the tax lever, double your real estate profit.

10. You do not have to be an expert to get returns on your real estate investments

Very true. In fact, Warren Buffett is not an expert in real estate, let alone an expert in farms or shopping centres. So, how did you invest and achieve these results even if you are not an expert? The reason is simple. Warren Buffett knows the rules of investments and applies them in all fields: on the stock exchange, in real estate, in the business. Warren Buffett knows how to recognize an investment opportunity, take action, and close a big deal.

That is why even a person who is not an expert in real estate can invest and earn a lot because you do not need to be an expert, but you must know the rules of the game or the basis of the investment. These can be learned by anyone, even from those who do not believe it is possible to learn them. The next step is to put these notions and strategies into practice. The result? You will get results, just like Warren Buffett has been doing for decades. Not a bad perspective, right?

But is real estate a great place to invest your money?

On this topic, I think that one of the most repeated phrases is:

"Brick is an excellent investment. It is safe and never betrays. The value of the property always grows over time ".

But as you probably noticed, you are not exactly like that, as the price of houses has fallen considerably over the last few years.

We must, therefore, try to overcome popular beliefs and give an adequate answer to the questions namely:

Is it still worthwhile investing in properties today?

And to solve this doubt, we cannot rely on "hearsay" or "bar opinions", but we must rather rely on a serious and documented analysis of how things really are.

Every time I talk to someone with money, in 99% of cases, we end up talking about real estate.

"That one is so rich that he owns the whole city"

"That guy collects an avalanche of money every month through his properties."

These and other similar discourses are generally used to indicate the wealth of people who, in the popular imagination, have built a fortune thanks to the brick.

Investing in real estate: a safe investment after all?

If you talk about buying a big car, many may wonder if you actually can afford to keep it.
If you go on vacation with a certain frequency, someone mumbles that you are a spendthrift.

Even worse, if you rely on an independent financial advisor or if you open a trading account to make investments, they immediately label you as crazy!

However, if you declare that you have bought a $250,000 apartment to go and live or if you have purchased a property that is falling apart in the suburbs of the world, compliments are in abundance and nobody doubts the goodness of your choice.

This is because we are used to thinking that real estate investment is as safe as a government bond.

"The grandfather has paid the house 2 million, today it is worth 200,000 dollars" (inflation, for heaven's sake, let's not go down that route please!).

Here is just one of the many data that you can check yourself on the progress of our "safe investment" from 2007 to 2019.

The value of real estate has literally plummeted over a single decade (-28% in the best case).

Probably, we are touching the fund and then go back, but the fact remains that those who bought in the pre-economic crisis, i.e. in the collective euphoria of the race to the brick, today saw the value of its investment strongly depreciated.

Who has had the need to get rid of their purchase has literally sold off or has remained with the weight on the rump for years, given the absence of a flourishing market ready to win the apartment.

The old reasoning on the security of real estate purchase collides with the harsh reality of the world that has changed significantly.

If your relatives bought in the post-war period, when there was a company to be rebuilt from scratch and so many cities practically did not exist, it is quite obvious to say that there has been a re-evaluation.

First, there were the stones, 30 years later, there were cities. Until the 70s, the population was young and procreated at great rates. From the 1990s onwards, population growth, in line with other Western countries, has been miserably arrested, only to reverse the trend.

We are always the same, we are older and there are no more avalanches of people and families willing to move, change cities, and enrich the demand for apartments.

According to The American Institute of Public Opinions, 80% of Americans today live in a house owned, that is, the same Americans who are old, and therefore do not move, do not have children and, all in all, can always stay in the first apartment in which they entered. In a nutshell, anyone who could buy a house has already done it.

All others are either not owners by choice or simply cannot afford it and must live in rent.

The legislation on leases, among other things, is very unbalanced in favor of the tenants and getting a bad guy, in a historical era of changes and difficulties in employment, has become more frequent than anything else.
All this leads to a dutiful reflection.

If almost everyone has a home in which to live, if we are on average less young and less likely to travel, if we have now almost poured near large urban centres leaving the suburbs, how can we think of a growth propulsive real estate market in the coming decades?

Well, now that I slapped you and I made you understand why the adage "the brick is a safe investment" is a commonplace of the past; we can try to understand when it becomes convenient by doing two calculations together.

Also, because the fact that it is not so sure does not mean that there are no opportunities to be seized.

In investing in real estate, opportunities are there and will always be there. I want to warn you before entering the heart of the discussion. After a brainstorming of negative things, we come to the opportunities that the sector offers at this time.

First point: prices are at historic lows.

The collapse of prices can be a pain for those who sell, but an opportunity for those who buy.

Every market has its own precise movements and lives of ups and downs and even the real estate is not immune to all this. Specifically, in the real estate market, there are many people who, unfortunately, must sell because they have immediate liquidity needs.

If we add this aspect to the already huge amount of property in circulation, this means that, as there is so much offer, you can buy at relatively low prices compared to the past.

From this point of view, many innovations are spreading also in America.

Short-term rentals are on the rise thanks to the explosion of portals such as Airbnb and Home Away. Thanks to the diffusion of cheap means of transport, people who go on holiday have increased considerably and do not disdain to stay in apartments rather than in hotels. Tourism in our country, overall, is in excellent health. According to the MIBACT statistical office, last year, we exceeded the threshold of 50 million visitors and recorded an increase of about 5 million visitors compared to 2018.

Although our universities are not among the best in the world, they attract students from all over the country. From the outskirts to the cities, from the South to the North, every year, many off-site students move to get their degree. In short, the question is there, but obviously, it is necessary to act selectively to grasp the potential that only some areas, and not all without distinction, can offer.

The main tourist resorts will never go into crisis and the short rental market is quite benevolent with the owner because he does not have the familiar difficulties.
Large cities attract tourists, students, and workers who generally offer greater guarantees and with whom it is possible to sign contracts with shorter duration and, therefore, less exposed to the risks of residential rent.

Above all the centres of big cities are often the object of a secular development with respect to the suburbs, which become impoverished and depopulated.

People, especially wealthy people, prefer services to the isolation of remote areas.

In short, investing in real estate is still possible, if you know how to do it!

Investing in real estate: let's do the maths!

I want to share with you the analysis I did in the summer of 2017, thinking about New York. My hypothesis is based on the purchase of a property located in a strategic area because it is very close to the main university.

The idea of exploiting the investment is based on renting out-of-town students who come to the city to study. The area I am talking about is well served by public transport and is quite lively from a commercial point of view. The district is largely inhabited by families, the elderly, workers, or students. The rental market can be said to be good enough for the reason that ruled my choice.

Speaking of numbers, the price per square meter varies from $1,000 for properties to be completely renovated up to $1,800 for apartments in good condition and ready to be inhabited. Wanting for a moment to estimate to be good negotiators, we can concretely think of bringing home a two-bedroom apartment to renovate with $50,000. Obviously, we are also building experts and we select an apartment that is in good condition. You do not have to redo the systems, you just have to repaint, you have to replace the sanitary, and you have to change the floor in one of the rooms.

In light of my experience, I can tell you that the cost of the work is around $10,000.

We set a maximum ceiling of $8,000 and let us venture to IKEA.

To finance the operation, I stick to what all the books say about financial growth: select the mortgage which, among other things, is given to you at a very low rate.

If you are an entrepreneur like me and sometimes you have to come to the bank to ask for money, you know exactly what I am talking about. The bank will finance 80% of the work, because today, 100% mortgages are rare if you do not have a particular past history. However, since we are good and credible, the bank also finances the work partly, so on $60,000 of spending, we receive a loan of $48,000. I tried to pull down estimates for a twenty-year mortgage and the lowest provides a monthly payment of $234.95 in 20 years, with costs of investigation of $850 and appraisal for $320

To this, you must add other additional expenses such as:

1. Compulsory house cover: the annual cost that I estimate is about $240 which makes $4,800 for 20 years;
2. Life insurance: bad luck aside, one cannot be exposed to the risk of leaving debts to the heirs. I estimated a cost based on my age (27 years) and a capital of $50,000. I assure you with about $80 per year ($1,600 total in 20 years), if you have a few years more than me, you could pay a little 'more;
3. Disability coverage: For me, safety comes first. I never went around with the scooter because I was afraid of falling. Imagine if I buy a house with the risk of not having the money to make up for the diseases. Here, too, I made the estimate on myself and took out an annual cost of about $150, then $3,000 total over 20 years of a mortgage.

Calm, it's not over yet. At these expenses, you must add:

- Real Estate Agency commission: on a purchase of this type, you must estimate at least $3,500;
- Notarial deed: the costs are at your expense, you must pay both the deed of sale and the deed of a loan. At least $4,000 are needed;
- Registry tax: in short, if you buy as a first home, pay less. But, as an investment, we must rule out this hypothesis because you will not go there to live. The purchase, therefore, you do it as a second home and,

therefore, pay 9% that corresponds to $4,500.

To sum up, the total cost of the operation is:

- $56.388 (total to be returned to the bank) +
- $8,000 (furniture) +
- $850 (preliminary investigation) +
- $320 (appraisal) +
- $4,800 (home coverage) +
- $1,600 (life insurance) +
- $3,000 (disability coverage) +
- $3,500 (agency) +
- $4,000 (notary) +
- $4,500 (registration tax) = $86,958

Without going into the merits of what you have to pay right away and what are the extensions over time, the operation costs you $4,337.90 per year (total divided into 20 years of mortgage), i.e. $362.33 per month.

Now, we calculate the expenses of your competence, i.e. those that you must take out of your pocket and immediately:

9. $12,000 (advance 20%) +
10. $8,000 (furniture) +
11. $1,170 (appraisal and investigation) +
12. $3,500 (real estate agency) +
13. $4,000 (notary) +
14. $4,500 (taxes) =
15. $33,170 is the capital you need to start the operation.

Now that we have done the calculations on the expense, we come to the lease of the property.
We want to make it to students, so in the two-room apartment, we create two beds that we make at $350 each, for a monthly income of $700, which makes $8,400 gross annual income.

Let us simplify and pretend to rent without an agency, the costs charged to us are the dry coupon, which immediately declines 21% of the rent (which falls to $6.636) and condo and maintenance fees that, again to simplify, I esteem in $1,500 per year.

There is $5,136 net.

Considering the weighted annual cost, the net profit is $788.10 ($5.136 - $4.347.90).

You have taken out the loan for the purchase, letting you lend the money from the bank. In this case, the calculation on the return of the real estate investment must be based on the actual return generated by your capital, net of the instalment to be paid to the bank.

Technically speaking, we are talking about ROE that is the acronym of Return on Equity, where "equity" is the Capital. That is the one that you pour from your own pocket.

The calculation of the ROE is done with this formula:

(Net Annual Income/Own Capital) * 100

We calculate the Net Annual Income:

$5.136 - $2.819.40 (mortgage payment) - $470 (annual cost of insurance) = $1.846 annuity.

As for Capital, you have spent $33,170 to start everything.

So, if we put the data in the formula, we find: (1.846/33.170) * 100 = 5.56%

Congratulations, you have earned 5.56% on your investment property and you did better than American government bonds that do not reach 2%.

Am I wrong or have you read something similar even in the

newspapers?

Well, they're all false information and I'll explain why.

Investing in real estate: it is a profession, not an investment

As I begin to write this last paragraph, I look at the clock: 2 hours have passed since I started to reckon.

It took 2 hours just to plan, I dare not imagine even the time it would take if I wanted to do it in practice.

If you are an entrepreneur or a professional, you are used to reasoning according to the time value of your time, so just try to calculate the amount of hours needed to plan, organize, and manage all this, which can generate (when and if all goes well) an income of around $2,000 per year.

And I have not even tried to imagine the value of income if, instead of going to the bank, I had bought with my own money.

At this point, you could tell me that my calculations are wrong because you would be able to cut many expenses and maximize profits.

The difference between an investment and a business activity lies in the time it takes. I invest my money to make it work for me, I can even help a professional who drives me but, basically, I do not use 50, 100, or 200 hours per year to follow my investments.

If you take all this time to pursue investment, you are an industry professional or an entrepreneur and you are working exactly as I am now working on preparing this article. Furthermore, I have shown you the hypothesis in which the investment forecast is right.

The reality is clearly much more complex and often full of contingencies and (small or large) errors of assessment. With
36

all the variables we have seen, the chances of loss are not so remote. Moreover, since this is a business activity in all respects, the risks are high, as they must justify the potentially high returns.

Are you still sure that investing in brick is a safe and sound deal?

As you can see, once the fog blanket and the ham on the eyes have been removed, it is immediately clear that this is an operation that has its degree of complexity, as well as a certain amount of (right) risks.

As such, you must treat it in the same way you approach your work.

You have to spend time, a lot of time, to do your analysis, the checks, the calculations of the case, and the resolution of the small problems that will inevitably arise.

Furthermore, you must also bear the burden of "entrepreneurial" risks linked to the particular dynamics of this type of market.

Having said that, we have seen that there are still opportunities, even if they have to be selected with greater attention and precision than in the past.

Chapter 3: Master your Emotions

Loss aversion is based on the fact that investors are more afraid of losing than it is a pleasure to make money. Consider the classic experiment of choice, following the investment of 1,000 Euros:

1. I have a 50% chance of earning 200 Euros and a 50% chance of losing 100 Euros.
2. I have a 100% chance to earn 50 Euros.

In both cases, the expected return is 50 Euros, but most people will be oriented towards B. Note that even decreasing the amount of income in case B, many will continue to prefer it to A, regardless of whether the yield expected is both lower!

If we combine the effects of selective perception and loss aversion, it is easy to understand why many investments are kept for too long while those in surplus are too prematurely discontinued.

Aversion to losses and risk. Paradoxically, when faced with a loss, the aversion is so strong that the investor tends to take greater risk to offset it. This behaviour is very similar to those who in gambling lose large sums because "they cannot stop at a loss and want to make up".

The gambler's syndrome can be avoided with two moves: you decide how much you want to devote to riskier investments and you communicate it to an external controller (spouse, financial advisor, or friend) who has the moral authority to impose discipline and respect for the plan. Regarding the downsizing of risk appetite after unfortunate incidents, it is necessary to remember that, contrary to what our nature suggests, the markets are less risky the worse their recent performance was and that it makes no sense to buy insurance coverage (read financial products with protected and guaranteed capital) after the damage has occurred.

Costs and expenses are variable to be evaluated carefully. Their impact on the final result of investment far exceeds the intuition. Consider, for example, the case of a mutual fund, one of the most widespread investment vehicles and, to be fair, less expensive and more transparent. This tool exposes to explicit costs and implicit costs. The former is directly borne by the subscriber and can be quantified with precision. Basically, these are entry and exit fees, unjustified taxes and luckily applied more and more rarely. The implicit costs are borne by the fund itself, therefore, affect the operating result and are difficult to quantify, if not carefully analysing the prospectus. Here are the main ones:

1. Management fees. They range from 0.30% of funds, to 1.50% of bond funds, to 2% of equity funds. They are used to remunerate both management (choice of securities, administration of fund assets, calculation of the daily value of the portfolio, the activity of substitute tax), and placement (promoters, employees at the counter).
2. Custodial bank fees. Quantifiable in about 0.10%. They are used to remunerate the company that holds the fund's securities and verifies that the operations decided by the manager comply with the regulations.
3. Miscellaneous expenses. Difficult to quantify and to justify.
4. Performance Fees. They vary according to the performance obtained, and therefore, it is impossible to evaluate a priori. For an equity fund, in a year of positive returns, they may account for 0.20% to 0.40%.
5. Securities purchase and sale costs. Unable to know precisely, they represent the commissions paid by the fund to financial intermediaries. It can be estimated in the order of 0.20-0.30% per year.

Annual expenses are likely to reduce the return on an equity fund by 3%. A numerical example can help you understand what this means in terms of the final result of the investment. We hypothesize three different investment alternatives, identical in all but for costs: absent in the first, equal to 0.50% of the assets in the second, and equal to 2.5% in the third.

What will be the final result (upright, in technical terms) of an investment in a single solution of 10 thousand Euros, lasting twenty years, with an annual yield of 8%? Over 46 thousand Euros in the first case, 42 thousand in the second, and 29 thousand in the third.

That is, considering only the second and third hypotheses (no investment can be made without costs): a seemingly insignificant cost difference represents the difference between quadrupling or triple the initial capital. In practical terms, it is worth underlining that the two hypotheses examined correspond to the use, for social security purposes, of a category pension fund (low-cost alternative) or of an insurance pension plan (high-cost alternative).

The issue of costs is even more interesting if one examines the insurance products that provide for the notorious uploads, or the collection, by the insurance company, of a substantial part of the premium paid by the insured. Let us examine two hypotheses: the same initial investment (10 thousand Euros), the same holding period (10 years), and the same return (5% per year).

Various expenses: 0.50% per annum the first and 1.50% per annum the second, which also provides for a 5% charge (in other words, only 9,500 Euros are allocated to the investment, while 500 are spent on expenses). The upright of the first alternative will be €15,500, while in the case of the second; it will come to no more than €13,500. The difference of 2000 Euros corresponds to 15%.

Chapter 4: The Power of Diversification

With an initial example that could help to clarify the mind of newbies, try to hypothesize two distinct situations: in the first, the trader has filled his portfolio of only stock shares of the Alfa Company for 100,000 Euros; in the second, the trader filled the same value of the portfolio (100,000 Euros) with 100 different securities for an amount of 1,000 Euros. It is clear that in the first situation, the future of the trader will depend exclusively on the performance of the Alfa Company, with the risk that a negative trend in the price of Alfa shares will seriously affect the value of the portfolio; in the second case, the risk will be mitigated by the weighted performance of the 100 securities purchased.

In short, it should be clear that "diversifying" means investing in more markets, more financial instruments, and more assets, tending to differ from one another in nature, characteristics, and level of risk, in such a way that future of your portfolio does not depend on a single investment.

The more experienced traders will have clearly identified a voluntary error in the example above. And they can remind you that the degree of diversification does not depend so much on the number of financial instruments that you put in your portfolio but on their nature and their correlation. In other words, in order to obtain a diversified portfolio, it will not be necessary to include as many financial instruments and underlying assets as possible, as to examine their nature and the existing correlation. But what is the correlation?

We talk about correlation (positive or negative) between two financial instruments when they tend to move in the same direction (positive correlation) or vice versa (negative correlation). For our purposes, it is appropriate to make sure that the correlation is always very low (considering that today, a non-existent correlation is a semi-utopia) so that the returns of the financial instruments can mature independently from each other.

In fact, when a portfolio is not very diversified since their components are too positively correlated with each other, the risk that the entire portfolio goes into a loss at the same time is much higher. Not even the negative correlation is opportune: in the negative correlation hypothesis, in fact, the entire profitability of the portfolio could be compromised, since the gains of a financial instrument could correspond to the same losses of the other. Precisely for these reasons, it is good to build a well=diversified portfolio, where the correlations are at minimum terms.

What advantages brings a good diversification of the investment portfolio

As stated above, the benefits of a good risk diversification are mainly two: low volatility, greater protection against drawdown risk, and better return on investment. Let's see them separately.

Low volatility

The volatility is understood as the movement speed of the underlying, i.e. the percentage change in the quotations of a financial instrument in relation to a unit of time measurement (for example, the year). It follows that the higher the volatility, the greater the potential variation of the financial instrument in a given period of time. The weighting of the volatility of the various financial instruments in a portfolio will determine the volatility of the entire portfolio.

Drawdown

It is the loss of invested capital determined by the negative performance of a financial instrument or by the set of financial instruments present in the portfolio. If the portfolio is not well diversified, the risk of incurring significant and sudden drawdowns is much higher.

More profitability

Portfolio diversification leads to better returns/earnings as investments will be better protected. It follows that the portfolio will survive without serious disturbances to the moments of negativity, seizing instead the opportunities to maximize the gains in favourable moments, without increasing the risks.

Is it possible to diversify the portfolio in copy trading?
At this point, the time has come to make a more advanced focus on the possibilities to diversify their portfolio in copy trading, or in the trading mode that "copy" the actions of a trader "guru". Naturally, the possibility exists and is easily applicable in all the main copy trading systems in the most well-known brokers in circulation, such as eToro. But how to do it?

How to diversify to reduce risk

The steps are few but fundamental.

1. Diversify the trading style:

It should be well-known that investing with copy trading means copying the operations of other traders. Considering that on the social trading platforms the trader gurus to be copied are thousands, choosing the "best" could be difficult. So, try to understand how your points of reference think, how they operate if they apply constant strategies, and what financial instruments they use.

2. Diversify the underlying assets:
Once you have chosen the financial instruments on which to invest and on which to build your portfolio, you must try to identify the underlying assets that are most useful for our purposes. For example, if we choose to devote a significant part of our portfolio to Forex, we will have to choose currency pairs, if we choose to dedicate a part to CFDs, we will have to

choose which stocks, stock indexes, or commodities to bet, and so on.

3. Diversify leverage:

The third step, perhaps more difficult, is to diversify the leverage that is used to replicate the trading signals generated by traders and investors included in their portfolio. The advice is of course not to exaggerate with leverage since you would end up with having in your hands a portfolio that is not easily manageable and potentially very risky. Furthermore, the financial leverage is distributed on the basis of the operational characteristics of the trader's strategy, using leverage as an element of variation (decreasing or increasing) of the overall risk level.

In principle, bear in mind that even for the most experienced traders and for the most experienced strategies, the best practice is to never exaggerate with the lever, since an error (even a technical error), or an unforeseen failure of the strategy, could seriously prejudice the portfolio that drives leverage.

Financial leverage

We have already seen this as a third step to diversify our portfolio. Now, we analyze it in order to diversify its investment in the best possible way.

In fact, Financial Leverage is one of the most "delicate" aspects related to the management of its investments. Let's start by remembering that unless you have perfect awareness of your own resources, exaggerating with leverage is never advisable, as it could generate significant consequences (not always positive!) in terms of volatility and drawdown in the portfolio.

However, the above must not deviate from the possibility of benefiting from the leverage effect. In short, compatible with the first 2 points that we have had the opportunity to examine, try to understand if the social and copy trading with a trader from a bit aggressive strategy can still be integrated into your desires, perhaps looking - at the same time - to lower the

44

leverage assigned to be able to weigh the risk on your liking.

Chapter 5: Fundamental News That Impact the Market

The fundamental analysis in Forex, together with the technical analysis, is the best method of study for everything that happens on the financial markets, we talk about investigations without which the traders would find themselves lost.

Aware of the importance of the subject, we decided to provide you with a good preliminary guide to the fundamental analysis on the stock market, a small vademecum to consult every time you have forgotten an important notion and you realize that the time has come to refresh it. We hope that you take 5 minutes of the precious time you have available to get to the end and understand the rudiments and the importance of an analysis that really has a central role in the daily life of every trader willing to live professionally his business.

The fundamental stock market analysis can be completely useless if you do not use appropriate investing platforms. In fact, only the best investing platforms guarantee a good trading experience. What are we referring to? We are talking about authorized platforms, therefore platform that is honest and convenient, so without commissions and completely free. An example of a recommended stock investing platform is Plus500, one of the most popular platforms for traders in Europe.

The fundamental analysis in the stock market is also called "macroeconomic analysis". Industry professionals use this type of study to be able to predict time frames of medium and long periods such as prices of goods, securities, and currencies on international markets, just like stocks. Fundamental analysis is always carried out by professional analysts who are able to describe economic events and imagine the repercussions they have and will have on the stock market. Let's get more specific in the paragraphs that follow.

Macroeconomic investigations are studies on the "macroeconomic" causes that have the ability to influence the demand and the supply of currencies on the world's largest market of all (the stock market), as also on all the others possible and imaginable markets (the forex market, for instance).

The fundamental analysis in the stock market focuses both on the general economic situation of a given nation, but also on the global economic situation, but sometimes, also only on certain groups of States and goes on to identify the relationships that exist between them. The market functions as a whole, an inseparable totality of factors that move together in a correlated manner. Changes in the economy will, sooner or later, have their own specific weight on the trend in demand and supply of Forex currencies, as well as on commodities and stocks.

The interesting thing is that the stock market not only discounts all the economic changes that occur but of course, also political decisions play an important role in the performance because they are directly related to the economic results of the national entities. Also, when the correlation is not so direct, politics maintains a very important weight on the progress of the stock market. Not even the social aspects and the potential impact of climate change on trade in currencies should be underestimated.

It seems incredible and yet all these factors must be taken into consideration to make precise analyzes that will then lead to concrete and more than satisfactory results when it comes to making an investment.

The fundamental analyst is born as a figure in the stock market, that of the shares issued by large companies such as Microsoft, Apple, and Amazon. When a fundamentalist pose to the analysis of the potential of a company and defines it, its secondary task then is to consider what will be the future value of the shares of that company comparing it with the current market value.

Analysts make budget assessments that are published after being concluded with precision and caution. When an authoritative analysis is made known, it is bound to greatly stimulate the upward or downward movement of the prices of the company under examination. Obviously, the analysis is not made by the insiders of the companies but by external people who have to fulfill their duty in the most objective ways without making up the results.

Thanks to the analysis that you can make and those that are published online, you can decide how and when to invest in the stock market as well as all the other markets available on the net. Simply following the analysts' forecasts, you can speculate greatly on the upward movements or downwards which are caused by the positive and negative forecasts published.

Good practice for any fundamental analyst is to specialize in certain sectors of the economy and finance to understand which the most relevant data to consider are. In this way, with the experience that is matured over time, you can easily understand which ones the repercussions on the markets of certain events are. It is no coincidence that the best friend of the fundamental analyst is the notebook accompanied by a pen to write down the date of the event.

The markets are cyclical and react similarly to certain events, so this makes them predictable to some extent. It is this that fills with security and hopes anyone who operates in the stock market and is a technical or fundamental analyst.

Now, we want to go into more detail about what are the economic indicators that fundamental analysts keep in strict control to do their own type of analysis. The indicators we will talk about are important because you have to look at them every time you want to understand how a stock will behave and whether its value will be up or down compared to those of other countries.

You have certainly already heard of economic indicators. These data are statistical numbers measured over a period of time and provide growth estimates for the following months. The information produced by them is exploited, above all, by those who trade with the fundamental analysis method. The set of results of one or more indicators suggest an improvement or a worsening of the economic situation and are useful for determining your future strategy.

The study of macroeconomics is very complex and fascinating at the same time, because different factors can influence a given. The data are simply based on expectations of future growth or production. These data are not only used for investing, but are considered by national governments to make economic decisions. Following the publication of macroeconomic data, high volatility situations may occur in the market, which represent ideal situations for those who like to make profits on the stock market, especially on an intraday basis.

Gross domestic product or GDP: how many times on the news you have heard about GDP? GDP is nothing more than the gross domestic product of a country or the most important indicator of its present and future economic situation. GDP is certainly the most important macroeconomic data and we must always watch it to do serious business on the stock exchange. The GDP data is published every quarter, and then 4 times a year, its calculation undergoes adjustments. GDP is the sum of all goods and services produced by a nation throughout the year. If the GDP is positive, it means that the given economy is strong and healthy and leaves us well foreseeable for future events, if instead the GDP shows the minus sign or it stands at 0, it is not a good data and it can testify an oncoming recession.

Employment data. Employment data provide information on what a country's workforce is as it is distributed and what the forecasts are for the future. This data shows how many jobs have been lost and how many have been earned, but it also shows the number of people who become a "burden" for the state by applying for unemployment benefits. When the economy runs the right way, there are no problems with unemployment, the value of GDP increases, and people are all employed or at least the vast majority of it.

Inflation. Enormous importance for the stock market lies in the inflation value. The value of inflation is another important macroeconomic indicator because this value is measured through the Consumer Price Index and the GDP deflator. If nominal GDP is higher than real GDP, price increases are recorded on the market. Inflation is related to the purchasing power of currency and affects its exchange value in proportion to other currencies. If the economy is developing, the consumer price index increases and interest rates increase. The currency, therefore, acquires a higher value.

Balance of payments: in this case, we talk about the difference between the income and the exits of foreign currency against the national currency. It is determined jointly by the "import-export" balance and by the movement of capital. A negative value can, therefore, be caused both by imports higher than exports, a typical sign of overvaluation of the currency, and by capital flight, a typical indication of a lack of confidence in the stability of the currency and in the future of the country. In general, when payments received in the state budget exceed those sent, then things turn well and the currency should be strong.

Public debt: this is a further cause for concern for all Americans who hear that the news is increasing and the data is indeed worrying for a country that cannot stop its growth. Basically, it represents the total value of the debt accumulated over the years by a State and generally financed by the issue of government bonds. It should not be confused with the "deficit", which is the excess of outgoings on revenues in just one year. In the Treaty of Maastricht, a public debt exceeding 60 percent of GDP is considered excessive.

As you could see, there are not just a few data to consider in order to do fundamental analysis, but they are all important, especially those that we have listed, which are not even all those that should actually be consulted to get a clear picture of the situation.

In any case, a great help to make the fundamental analysis turns out to be the MacroEconomic calendar, that is easily available online, which shows all the news and the relevant dates of important news that can have an effect on the markets. Already, by simply consulting the economic calendar, you can trade with more awareness as long as you know the results that certain news will have on the stock exchange. Otherwise, it is almost useless to read this calendar. Trading and investing with fundamental analysis is a technique that offers excellent results and we highly suggest you try it out.

Chapter 6: Day Trading Penny Stocks

Investing is something that many people are interested in. They want to see how much their money can grow for them and some even want to see if they can make this a full-time income rather than working their regular jobs. There is a variety of investments that you are able to make. Some people keep it safe and place their money in a savings account while others go with a retirement plan. Some will go with real estate and choose one of those options when the market is good and others like to start their own business, get into the stock market, or invest in a friend who is doing something new. The options can be endless when it comes to starting a new investment, and picking out the right one for you can be the hardest part of getting started.

One investment type that you may want to try is the penny stock. This is a type of stock that starts out really low, at no more than $1 for each of the shares. According to the Securities and Exchange Commission in the United States, a penny stock is one that will trade at no more than $5 a share, but most of them will be less than that.

A penny stock can bring about a huge profit to those who know how to use it, but it is not a popular option as it works off the regular stock market and is often used when a company is really desperate for some money. There is the potential for large losses, even if you make the purchase at a small rate, but if you are able to read the market, there is the potential to see a great deal and make a good profit in the process.

One of the best ways to ensure that you aren't taking a big loss on these stocks is to be careful who you purchase from. There are some unscrupulous people who will make a big purchase of penny stocks in order to help raise the price. They will use fake press releases, websites, stock message boards, and more to talk up the penny stock so more people will make a purchase and then the price goes up even more. Then they sell the stocks at the inflated price, making themselves a lot of money while everyone else will not be able to find any buyers and will either have to hold onto the stock or sell it at a loss.

The good news is that the penny stock does need to meet some standards in order to prevent the process above, which is known as pump and dump. Inside the United States, these stocks need to have a price, market capitalization, and minimum shareholder equity. Remember that even if the stock you are looking at is below $5, it will not be a penny stock unless it is traded off of the stock exchange.

The good about penny stocks

We spent a little time talking about some of the things that you will need to avoid when using penny stocks and looking to invest in these opportunities. If you are careful about watching the market and seeing what is going on before you make a purchase, you should be able to figure out when a pump and dump scheme is going on. If something looks like it is rising in price too quickly, you see that there was only one buyer of a large number of penny stocks with just one company, or you feel like this person is really trying to pressure someone into making a purchase that doesn't look like the best, it is a good idea to go with a different option for the penny stocks.

The good news is that you are able to do well in penny stocks. You just have to keep your head and make sure that you aren't trying to rush into something that doesn't make sense or that has a lot of red flags all over it. One of the best ways to get the most out of your penny stocks is to learn how to do your research before making any purchases.

There are many things that you will be able to research about a penny stock before you get started. For example, start by looking at the corporate website for the company you want to work with. This provides you a good idea about the company because a lot of information can be there. You should then look at the balance sheet of the company to see how many debts the company is dealing with; if there are too many debts, the company may be trying to sell the penny stocks to get out of debt, but if they haven't learned how to control that debt, throwing more money over to them will not help. You want to pick penny stocks out from companies that are profitable or the ones who are able to properly reduce their losses and will not take on large amounts of debt to keep running.

Penny stocks can be a great form of investing if you are looking to get started with an option or you want to expand out your portfolio to make your money work a little harder. We are going to take a look at more parts about penny stocks and how you will be able to make them go to work for you.

So, before we get into some of the basics of trading in penny stocks, we need to take some time to understand the different methods that companies can list themselves in this kind of market. Remember that while there are rules for penny stocks, they are not considered part of the stock market so working with them is going to be a bit different than what you are used to. Here, we are going to talk about how a company is able to list in Pink Sheets and what this means for you the investor.

Listing in Pink Sheets

For a company to get started with penny stocks, they will first need to file Form 211 in order to be listed in Pink Sheets. This is a privately held corporation, compared to the other option (which we will talk about later) over-the-counter Bulletin Board, which is a service that is owned by the NASDAQ. There are many companies that use Pink Sheets to work with and when they fill out the Form 211, they will need to submit it over to the OTC Compliance Unit. The market maker is going to process the listing for the company. The broker and dealer will be able to quote a price for this company, as long as the company is pretty transparent. However, there are some companies that won't commit to this transparency because they won't submit their current information on business financials.

For the companies that are listed using the Pink Sheets, you will find that they are a small and thin trader. This company will not have to work with the SEC during the trading time and they don't have to file their periodic reports. Now, some of them will do this filing in order to show what they are doing and to help the investor feel more comfortable with working with them, but this is not a requirement. In many cases, it can be difficult to get information in order to understand companies that are on the Pink Sheets because you just don't have the information that is needed to get started.

The Benefits of Trading Pink Sheets

Despite the fact that the companies who use Pink Sheets are not required to be transparent or file periodic updates, an investor is usually going to find some pretty good options to trade in penny stocks with these Pink Sheets. You have the possibility of getting a high return because these are the stocks that are volatile. There are also some companies that are in this group that used to be strong, but for some reason or another, had to leave the major exchanges because of a strict requirement they no longer met. They may still be good companies to trade with and you could make some good profits from it.

It is also possible to find obscure companies to trade with in order to help that company grow before they move over to one of the major exchanges. You would be able to invest with these companies early on and this could give you a huge reward later as they start to grow and move over to the stock exchange.

In addition, the Pink Sheets system has a tier system that helps you to differentiate between the companies that are there. This helps you to figure out which stocks are higher risks and which ones are lower risks based on the classifications that are set. You are able to pick whichever risk setting that you are happy and comfortable with, but as a beginner, it is nice to know which ones fall into each category to help you make a decision.

If you want to use the Pink Sheets as part of your trading, you need to make sure that you really do your research. Pink Sheets is not going to provide you with much information about the companies you are trading with and if you just randomly pick a company, you are increasing your risk and making it likely that you will lose all of your money.

The Classifications System

As mentioned before, the Pink Sheets system has a classification for each of the companies that trade using it. This makes it easier to determine whether a company is a high risk or low risk and you can make your decisions based on this. Some of the tiers that are found inside of the classification system include:

Trusted tier

Inside of the trusted tier in Pink Sheets, you will find the international as well as American companies that are considered trustworthy and investor-friendly. The companies that are from other countries are going to be on the international exchange, but they can still fit into this trusted tier. The companies that are in this tier have not met the requirements to be on the regular stock exchange, but this is usually because of one or two small things since the stock exchange is so strict.

However, even though these companies were not able to get onto the stock exchange, they were able to pass an independent audit. This list sometimes does include companies in American that pass the standards needed for NASDAQ but they aren't submitting SEC reports and so they would be moved over to Pink Sheets instead.

Transparent Tier

This is a tier that will send in SEC reports, and sometimes, will also include those that are in Over-the-Counter Bulletin Boards. These are highly trusted companies because you will be able to see some of their financial reports as well as other information that is required for them to be good with the SEC. You will be able to do your research on these companies because it is provided to you and can save a lot of guesswork and hassle when choosing the penny stocks you want to work with.

Distressed Tier

Companies that are inside of this tier of Pink Sheets are ones that provide limited information for the investor to look at, and often, they are not following the guidelines that are set out by Pink Sheets. These companies may not even send out updated information to the SEC as they should, but some of them will work with the OTC disclosures. Not all of these are bad to work with, but sometimes, you need to be wary because they aren't sending out the right information and some of them have been bankrupt.

Dark Tier

This is the tier that you will really need to watch out for because it could cause some issues. Companies that are inside of this particular tier aren't sending in any information about their business. They aren't filing information with either the SEC or the OTC Disclosure service and they haven't done so over at least the last six months, making it really hard for the investor to have any idea how this stock is doing. There are some companies that get into this tier that are also failing with transparency in the market or they don't have a market marker.

Toxic Tier

As a new investor or any investor for that matter, it is best to stay out of the toxic tier. Companies that are in this tier will often rely on marketing strategies that are fraudulent such as using promotions that are questionable or sending out a lot of spam to name a few. These can also include some companies that are subjected to large corporate events that disrupt them or they may have a suspension by the government. In some cases, these will not actually have their own business operations and can be really dangerous to send your money to.

Taking a look at these different types of tiers inside this system can help you to make a more informed choice when it comes to working in the Pink Sheets. You will be able to see these rankings with any of the companies that you choose to go with and if you pick the one with the highest reputation, it becomes easier to get good returns on investments.

How to make decisions in Pink Sheets

So, now that we know a bit more about Pink Sheets and how they work, it is time to learn how to do the trading decisions. When picking out a penny stock that is inside of Pink Sheets, you are going to be limited to information and technical analysis of most of the companies. There are also some issues on occasion because there isn't a central exchange that you can use to buy and trade these stocks. This is why it is best to start out with a broker and dealer who will be able to walk you through this process.

As the investor, you will need to do a fundamental analysis of any company that you want to invest in, even if they are not sending the information your way. You can look at the different companies and their past history and you can look to see if there are some hidden gems that other people will miss out on right now, but which will make the stock better later on. With some good research, you will quickly be able to narrow down the choices that you want to use.

Working with Pink Sheets can be one way to get started on penny stocks, but you do need to be careful. Some of the companies are great and will provide you with information to pick them; many of these are working to get to the stock exchange, but for some small reason or another, they are not quite there yet and these are pretty safe options to go with. But there are also companies on the Pink Sheets that won't provide any information and some that are even fraudulent, so you need to be careful about the companies that you invest in to help keep your portfolio strong and growing.

Investing with OTC Bulletin Boards

Another option that you can choose to invest for your penny stocks is the Over-the-Counter Bulletin Boards or the OTC Boards. This one, at least inside of the United States, is operated through the Financial Industry Regulatory Authority and it will hold many of the stocks and securities that are not found on the NASDAQ or other stock exchanges. You will need to work with brokers and dealers in order to order the penny stocks since this is not an electronic method, and it can be pretty secure to work with.

This type of penny stock is usually seen as a little more secure because they are required to send in financial information and to be transparent. It is regulated a bit more, and often, the companies that are on this one will be here because they didn't meet some small requirement to be on the exchange. All of the companies that are listed on these bulletin boards will need to report their information to the SEC, but they don't have to include as much information as they would on the stock exchange and they can leave our information on their market capitalization, minimum share price, governance, and more.

These are usually seen as a bit more secure because of the fact that these companies have to send in information and report to the SEC while the companies on the Pink Sheets could do this reporting, but they didn't have to. Many beginners in penny stocks will choose to go with this option because it allows them to learn a bit more about the company that they want to invest in, making it easier to pick a smart investment on their end of things.

Both the OTC Bulletin Boards and the Pink Sheets can be great places to start in order to find the penny stock that you want to work with. Some of the options can be a bit risky, but as a good investor, it is up to you to step in and do the research to find this information out. You are going to find risky investments no matter where you are, whether on or off the stock market, or in other forms of investing, but you need to find the one that works the best for you and has the right risk to reward ratio that you are comfortable with. Both of these trading methods have their own systems to help you to make these decisions and if you are working with a broker and a dealer, you should have the support that you need to make the right decisions.

Now that you know a bit more about working with penny stocks, it is time to work on putting some money into the stock that you would like to use and making sure that you get the right stock that will help you to make the money that you would like from this option. This chapter is going to help you learn how to get started with the penny stocks so that you can see the profits that you want in no time.

Opening your account

So the first step for you to do when starting on penny stocks is to pick out and open up a trading account. As an investor, you need to consider how easy the account is to work with. You should think about how easy it is to transfer the accounts to and from the account, the customer service with the account, and any fees that are associated with opening and running the account. There are times when a broker will choose a fixed rate for a smaller number of shares but this rate can increase when you trade on more shares; depending on the type of trading that you do, this could make a big difference in the profit that you make.

The nice thing about working on a commission per share idea is that it works well for investors who want to get into penny stocks but who don't have a lot of extra money for this. As the investor, you will need to shop around in order to find the best broker and the best trading account to help open up your options and maximize your profits so take the time to look at and talk to a few different companies to determine which one is the best for you to open up.

Picking out your penny stocks

When you are ready to find the penny stocks and make a decision, you will need to choose which one you want to use from the Over-the-Counter Bulletin Board or from the Pink

Sheets. You should be able to receive a list of the stocks that are available for you to use and you can do your research and pick the ones that you would like. Some brokers are able to provide you some screening tools so that you are better able to pick out the stock for your risk tolerance and your investing strategy.

Since penny stocks are a very volatile investment, it is possible to make a lot of money from your investment, but it is also possible to lose a lot of money in the process as well. This means that you need to never rush into the trades and you need to think some of them through.

There aren't a lot of people who invest in penny stocks, including money managers, index funds, and various mutual funds, which is one of the reasons that the penny stock market is going to be so volatile. Since there aren't many investors that go with this option, you may have times that there are liquidity problems. You may not be able to share some of the stocks that you own because there just aren't enough buyers available who would take the stock at all, much less at the price that you would like. You may have to take a big loss and really sell them at a low price in order to earn any money back, but it may be at a loss. But there is also a possibility that these stocks will go the other way and you are able to sell them at a much higher value than you purchased them. But it is the job of the investor to decide which way this is going to go before making a purchase of a penny stock.

Choosing a broker

A broker is an important person who will help you to get started on the penny stocks. A broker is going to be in charge of providing you with the platform that you need in order to work on your trades. They can work with you to provide some recommendations for what stocks to purchase, as well as providing marketing and sales services for all stakeholders. They will have a lot of tools and advice that you would be able to use when you get started. Every broker that you work with will have different services and tools that you can utilize, so this should go into consideration when it comes to picking out the broker you want to work with.

Many of the brokers you want to consider will have a good presence online and some will offer trading platforms that work on mobile devices. You can also work with some that offer bank accounts or nostro for trading these shares. No matter what method you are using for your trading and which one you think is best, it is important that you choose a broker who is able to provide you with reliable and instant money transfers so that you are able to complete your trades in the right time.

If your broker is slow at doing these transfers for you, you may end up losing out on a lot of money because you pay more than expected for the stock or they aren't quick enough at getting you out of the game so be careful with this when working with them.

Some other things that you should consider when picking out a broker are the fees and charges they are going to give to you. All brokers are going to want some fees to help pay them for doing their job, but learn right from the beginning how much they are going to charge you and what it all depends on (such as if they charge one rate for a small number of trades and then another rate for many trades). Always look at the terms and conditions on the website of your broker to see if you agree with everything that the broker will do for you as well as your own responsibilities.

Rules to ensure you make a profit when trading penny stocks

While there is going to be some risk when you go into penny stocks, there are a few rules that you will be able to follow to make it easier to make some money with penny stocks. Some of the rules that are best for your trading include:

1. The investor needs to have a plan in place right from the

start that helps them to know their entering and exiting strategy. This helps to keep some of the emotions out of the game.

2. The investor needs to know when it is time to exit. You should cut your losses when the market starts to become unpredictable so that you don't lose more money.

3. The investor needs to make sure that the reward is larger than the risk. You never should enter into a trade that seems like a sure loss.

4. The investor must have a good scheme for managing their money. They must always keep this in mind when picking out a penny stock.

5. The investor should never trade using their emotions. This is sure to lead to a big loss that will get worse when the emotions come into play. They must have discipline in emotional times and learn how to follow their plan of investment all the time.

6. The investor should avoid trading during the first hour of the day. There are many older investors who use this time to work on selling shares to beginners and they know that the price is going to go down. They hope to make a profit during this time before the stock goes down. So wait a few hours and then do your trading.

7. The investor should never invest more money than they are able to lose. This is a really risky option for investing and it is speculative. It is possible to earn a good profit if you are smart about your investments but never get so into the game that you invest more than you have to lose.

Learning to minimize your risks

When it comes to penny stocks, it is important to realize that this is a really risky way to invest your money. You are not working with items that are on the stock exchange, and sometimes, getting the information that you need in order to make informed decisions can be almost impossible to do. While you can make a lot of money with penny stocks, it is also possible to lose a lot of money in the process as well.

Luckily, there are some things that you are able to do in order to severely minimize your risk with penny stocks. There are a few things that you must watch out for because this help to show that a stock is too risky to work with. For example, if you notice that a company has a small operation and only a modest market capitalization, it is one of the riskier investments. Another thing to watch out for is stocks that sell too low. These stocks are going to trade at lower than $1 a share because these need to have a lot of caution so that the amount doesn't go lower.

Some people think that all big companies started out with penny stocks and this is why they choose to go into this kind of investment. There are a few that do start out as penny stocks to get the funds that they need before moving into the stock market, but this is abnormal and most do not work this way. So, why are some companies interested in offering these penny stocks when there are options? Some companies will go with the penny stock when they want to pay for something expensive in the company or when they are looking to expand. The company can offer the penny stocks in order to distribute some of its profits and make changes to its tax structure each year. Some brokerage firms will convince companies to offer up these stocks because the brokers want to earn some money from investors. Some companies will even offer these penny stocks if it determines that they are not going to grow anymore in the future and they would like to place the ownership on the investors.

This is why you need to be careful about the penny stocks that you get into. Some are just looking for some help to expand and they will be reputable options that you can make some money on if you are careful and do your research. But others are just trying to offload some of their responsibilities or they want to get a tax break, rather than help you out, and you could end up losing a lot of money. When you go into the penny stock, a good way to think about it is that these companies don't really care about the investor. If you have this wary thought in your head when investing, you are more likely to pick out a stock that benefits you the most.

Scams and penny stocks

Scams are pretty prevalent inside of penny stocks because they are not part of the normal stock exchange so they are pretty much lacking on rules. Many of the companies don't even follow the SEC rules or file with them well so getting information that you need can be difficult. It is easy for scams to arise in this situation.

As the investor, you need to be careful with your money and watch out for these scams. There are many good companies you can trade with and make some good money on, but there are also lots of bad brokers who will try to just take your money, bad companies that want to make money quick, and even other investors who will start buzz to bring up their own stocks and earn higher than they paid for a bad stock. You need to be independent and learn to think on your own so that you can get the best return on investment and not get taken in by one of the scams.

Getting started on penny stocks is pretty easy as long as you know which companies to trust, pick out a good trading account, and find a broker who will not charge you too many fees to work with. Add in some good research and one of the trading strategies that we will talk about below, and you are all set to making some great money with penny stocks.

Some misconception about the penny stocks

It is common for people who want to make money off these penny stocks to start spreading some rumors and misinformation about how penny stocks will work. It is likely that you have heard at some point that penny stocks were the way that many popular stocks on the market got started out. These rumors started in order to get new investors to purchase stocks that they wouldn't otherwise at a higher price because they want to be in on the ground floor of a company that is going to go big. However, as a diligent investor, you will find out that this is not true and the only reason that some of these companies had stocks that were worth less money is because they split up their stocks, not because they started out as penny stocks.

Some people also assume that because a company is in penny stocks, it is not safe to trade on at all. This is true in some cases; there are some companies who just want to make money quickly and then leave you with something that is worthless, but there are also some companies that are using this as a way to help them out. The regulations for getting on the stock market are pretty strict and some companies are really great, but miss out by a little bit for getting onto the stock market. They may start out on the penny stock while they work on making it to the stock market, but there is nothing fundamentally wrong with them. These are the companies that you will want to work with because they can make the best return on investment.

It is never a good idea to go into penny stocks thinking that it is easy. There are many brokers and others who are in this business who will try to tell you all their success stories and try to convince you that anyone is able to get into penny stocks and make a fortune. These people are usually trying to get you to buy into something so that they can make more money as well. Penny stocks are hard work and you need to keep at them and really do your research, not just listen to what another investor or a broker is telling you.

There are a lot of misconceptions that are out there about penny stocks. Some of them may be a little bit true, but many of them are just because of the buzz that is around the penny stocks to get you to purchase them or they are from people who just don't understand how the market works. Before you invest your hard earned money, make sure to take a step back and really understand how these kinds of stocks work so that you can make the best decisions possible.

There are two things that trading penny stocks are very much known for:

1. You can quickly make a big amount of money.
2. There is a high probability that you will lose your investment.

These are two opposing extremes that you will be facing. Of course, your objective is to rake in serious profits. Unfortunately, the majority of people who trade penny stocks fail to make any positive return. In fact, they lose their money. But do not be discouraged; because there are still people out there, the well-experienced and real expert traders who double, triple, and continuously grow their money more than you can ever imagine.

Losing trade is normal. Even well-experienced traders make the wrong investment decisions from time to time. However, you must avoid such mistakes as much as possible. Now, in order to help cut down your future losses, you should be aware of the risks that you will be facing when you trade penny stocks.

The Risks

Small Companies

The majority of the companies in the penny stock market are small companies. In fact, they can be so small that they do not even meet the minimum capitalization requirement. You will find many of these companies on the Pink Sheets. But then again, as discussed in the previous book, do not buy penny stocks from the Pink Sheets. Since they are small companies, it is hard to tell if they are stable enough and if they will even grow. Many small companies also tend to be less professional. Sometimes, the executives of a small company see and treat the assets of the company, including the stocks and penny shares, as their own personal belonging.

Start-Up Companies

Many of the companies that issue penny stocks are start-up companies. Therefore, they tend to have a very limited history that you can track. This makes it risky because you would not know for sure if the business is legitimate or if the company is operating a scam.

Less Transparent

Penny stocks do not have stringent requirements. You can always buy them on the Pink Sheets or over the counter (OTC). Remember that the companies on the Pink Sheets are not required to file with the SEC and to meet the minimum capitalization requirements or capital stock of a legitimate company.

Many companies on the Pink Sheets only reveal very limited information about their business, so it is hard to get sufficient and accurate data. Worse, some companies operate a scam.

Bankruptcy

The penny stock market is not only participated by small and start-up companies, but it also has companies that are about to go bankrupt. Unfortunately, these struggling companies will not reveal that they are already about to declare bankruptcy and will even make their stocks to look like an attractive investment. Of course, there is still a probability to make a good amount of profit when you invest in a company that is struggling to survive, especially when the company is able to save itself from bankruptcy and begin to grow successfully. However, the probability for such an ideal scenario to happen is small. Trading penny stocks are already risky enough; you would not want to take more risks.

The reason why you should not invest in a company that is about to go bankrupt is that you will run the risk of losing everything. Once the company declares bankruptcy and does not have sufficient assets to cover all its debts and obligations to its creditors, you will not be able to get your money back.

Low Liquidity

Penny stocks have low liquidity. With low liquidity, they become open to manipulation. A common type of fraudulent scheme is the pump and dump, in which the value of certain penny stocks are pumped up using some fraudulent marketing hype in order to convince traders to buy them. As its name already implies, the price of certain stocks is pumped up using some promotional or marketing hype. In turn, traders will find the stocks attractive and make an investment. The penny stocks are then dumped on the traders and their value begins to fall down.

Take note that the pump and dump scheme can be applied even if the company is actually doing well. In fact, when the company is making profits, the pump and dump scheme will be harder to detect. By adding a few dollars on the price of certain stocks that are already increasing, it is almost impossible for traders to determine whether the increased total value is due to legitimate means or merely a result of a pump and dump scheme.

Speculative

Due to so many factors that affect the prices of penny stocks, it can be said that the penny stock market is highly speculative. An important thing in trading penny stocks is to first buy the stocks that truly have a good value. Unfortunately, with the increasing number of scams, hackers, and frauds out there, it becomes difficult to know whether you are really purchasing a good stock or merely a stock whose value is being pumped. Second, even if you get to buy a profitable stock, there are many active factors that can affect its performance in the market. The best stock today may no longer be considered a good stock by tomorrow, depending on the circumstances. Also, granting that the prices of your penny stocks increase, will the buyers still see them attractive and profitable by the time you want to sell them?

These, among many other things, are the risks faced by traders of penny stocks. Consider also the sad fact that most traders fail to make any profit and simply lose their investment.

Do you think you are up for the challenge? If your entrepreneurial spirit is not crushed by these risks, then get ready for the awesome benefits of trading penny stocks.

The Benefits

Trading penny stocks are one of the best investment opportunities that offer wonderful benefits. So, if you honestly think that you can manage the abovementioned risks, then welcome to the world of high profits — a place where you can double, triple, or even multiply your money by more than 20 times in a short period of time.

Price

Penny stocks are cheap. A single penny stock only costs less than $5. If you have a lot of money to invest, then you can have thousands of stocks from different companies. If you are on a shoestring budget, then this opportunity is also available to you.

High potential return

When you trade penny stocks, there is a potential to multiply the value of your stocks many times over. In fact, there is a potential for the prices of your stocks to double within 24 hours or less.

Unlike blue-chip stocks where a 60% increase is considered a big profit already, such is considered normal when you trade penny stocks. And, unlike binary options where you can gain 90% but has a much higher risk, trading penny stocks can make your money grow by more than 500% within a short period of time. Also, since the penny stock market is mostly composed of small businesses, there is a high probability for the value of their penny stocks to grow, since small businesses have a lot of space for improvements.

High volume

You can have thousands of penny stocks for a small amount. Having a high volume of penny stocks is good, especially if you get them from a start-up company that is doing well.

Low or controlled risk

Penny stocks are inexpensive. You do not have to purchase a lot of penny stocks to earn a decent amount of profit. You can also diversify your stocks to help minimize your losses. And, unlike trading binary options where you will lose your whole wager when you make a wrong investment decision, you can still keep your penny stocks and sell them. If you are patient enough, there is really no such thing as a permanent loss. Considering the volatility of penny stocks, even if the value of your penny stocks decreases, there is a good chance that it will increase after some time.

Now that we have spent some time talking about penny stocks and how to get started on them and we did all the research, it is time to work on dealing with the penny stocks. If the stock is a good one (which you should be able to determine from the research that you did before), it is time to pick out the strategy that you are going to use in order to get started. Keep in mind that if you are going with a popular stock, the price is going to be high to start with and it can be hard to get started.

Before we look at some of the strategies that you are able to use with penny stocks, we need to remember that it is not a good idea to chase a stock. Chasing means that you will raise your buying price quickly because you are desperate to get the shares instead of someone else. This is a really bad thing to work with because your emotions are going to start running and you will often spend a lot more on the stock (and sometimes, it will be a bad stock) than it is worth. Eventually, the buyers who chased the stock will find that the value of the stocks will go down and the price will go the same way, making it hard to sell them at all, even for a loss.

One thing that you should remember is that it is important to pick out a strategy that you want to work with and then stick with it. Most of the strategies that are listed below, as well as some of the others that you may find or hear about in your work, are going to help you to make a good return on investment if you learn how to use them properly and you don't skip from one strategy to another.

Some beginners find that when they make a trade and it doesn't work while using one strategy, they will try to move over to another strategy and get this one to give them some of the results that they need. They assume that there was something wrong with that initial strategy and that they just need to try something else. The problem comes when they do this over and over again, switching strategies each time that something goes wrong.

This is an example of letting the emotions get in the way of what you want to do. If you are always switching out the strategy that you want to use, you are never really learning how to use one of them and your whole plan is going to become a mess. You need to pick one and really get to know it, understanding how it works from all angles and in all situations, in order to get the best results with your trading. Over time, you may find that it is better to get rid of one strategy and change it to another because the one isn't working or you find one will work better with your style, but it is never a good idea to skip around on the strategies that you are using all the time because it is just going to confuse you and makes it hard to ever see the success that you want with penny stocks.

The good news is that when you pick a strategy to work with inside of penny stocks, you are able to avoid the issues with chasing or some of the other issues that can come up when using penny stocks and trying to make a purchase. There are many strategies that you are able to pick from so you don't have to feel that you are only going to be able to use one and not feel comfortable with it. Some of the trading strategies that you may want to consider when working with penny stocks include:

Day Trading

When it comes to working with day trading, the investor is going to buy and then also sell their security in just one day, sometimes, doing it several times during this day with at least one of their stocks. Fortunes can be made with this kind of trading, but they can also be quickly lost. In order to get the day trading to work, you need to have a lot of experience and knowledge in your marketplace, a good strategy, and sufficient capital. You are not able to get into it at the last minute and you must be able to think clearly to keep your losses in check.

There are a number of benefits of going with day trading including:

1. The potential profits that you can earn will be huge if you get more than one trade that is profitable during the day.
2. The risk that comes with the stock or company changing is going to be reduced because you are not holding onto the stocks for that long. It is not likely that the company

is going to change in just a day.

There are also a few cons that come with the day trading option, which is one of the reasons that people choose to go with one of the other methods of trading. Some of the cons that you will find with day trading include:

1. You need to have an account balance that is pretty large before you can even get started.
2. For those who are not used to working in the stock market and who can't control their emotions well can quickly lose a lot of money.
3. Since you need to use a margin account, this type of trading can make you lose more money than you put in, which can be really dangerous in this option.

Momentum Trading

The next strategy that you may want to go with is momentum trading. This is a strategy that the investor would use if the stocks are moving quickly, as well as on a high volume, going in one direction. When it comes to penny stocks, many of the investors are going to play on an upward momentum because these are not usually going to be available for a short sale.

Stocks have momentum is because there is some buzz that is going on around the stock, such as through the news or because of rumors. To find these stocks, you will need to do some research and read through forums, message boards, and the news to find out what is going on. You should be able to find a few stocks that are getting quite a bit of attention at a time, which means that traders are going to be playing the stock pretty hard in order to get the price to go one way, and then they will take their profit before it all goes downward again.

There needs to be some research that goes into using this option. You need to take the time to watch how the activity for trading on the stock is doing before you make the purchase. Ones that have the potential to be done with momentum are ones that have a really high volume and stocks that are moving either much higher or in the opposite direction compared to the market. You will be able to watch out for these signs by looking at charts and watching the Level 2 quotes and the price action.

So, after you have a list of the stocks that you would like to use, it is time to make the purchase. You will want to purchase it as quickly as possible, at as low of a price as possible, before the momentum starts to go down again. Once you own the penny stock, you need to be ready to go, watching the changes in the market, looking at charts, and seeing if there are any new filings or news. If you see that there is anything negative about the stock, such as bad news, bad indicators, or a negative trend, you should try to do a quick sell to cut the losses before moving on; this is not an industry where you wait it out to see if it gets better.

On the other hand, if the momentum keeps going up, you will still need to hold on to the stocks and wait until some of the bids start to pile up. If the momentum is going up when you receive these bids and they are high enough for you to consider, you may want to go with one of them. The momentum can quit going up at any time and could start to go lower so take a bid that you are comfortable with before the tides start to turn. There may be a chance of earning more if you hold onto them longer, but if you hold on to long, you are going to lose it all so it is better to get what you can out of them.

Some of the benefits that you will be able to see with momentum trading include:

1. The penny stocks are often going to be the ones that move the most when momentum starts to move, which means that you are able to make a lot of money in a short amount of time.
2. You will be able to find a lot of information through message boards and other forums in order to pick the stocks that are right for you.

While this is a great way to make some good money in a short amount of time, there are also some cons that you will need to watch out for. Some of the cons of using momentum trading include:

1. Sometimes, the penny stocks are going to be volatile so your opportunity to sell and make a profit can be too short to earn anything.
2. Companies that have dilution agendas can sometimes stall out a momentum run.
3. There are some people who will use this idea in order to get more people to want their stocks. They will fake the buzz and the news so you need to be careful with working with them.

Swing Trading

Another option that you are able to work with is swing trading. This type of trading is good if you are working on a stock that has the potential to move around in a short time period. This is usually going to be for stocks that will move within the day but can go for up to four days. This is a type that will use technical analysis in order to look for a stock that may have momentum for their price over the short term. With this one, you are not going to be that interested in the values of the stock, but rather the trends and patterns of their price.

In a perfect market, the stocks are going to trade below or above a baseline value, or a moving average. The penny stocks are going to use this as both the resistance and support levels. When you are experimenting around with the charts, you will be able to see a set of moving averages will be fit to the actions of the price, and this can help out with the decisions during trading. Someone who has been in the stock market for some time would know that they should buy near the bottom of the moving average, but then they would sell before it reaches the target moving average.

There are quite a few pros that can come with this option

including:

1. This is a good style to use for beginners who are trying to get into the market and still makes some profits.
2. Home runs are not usually going to be done with swing trading, but if you catch the beginning of a new uptrend, there is the possibility of getting large profits.
3. You can use the basics of this kind of trading in any market that you would like. Big board stocks, futures, XCM, and Forex also use swing trading.

While there are quite a few positives that come with using penny stocks, there are also a few things that you need to watch out for. Swing trading is not an option that everyone is going to be fond of. Some of the cons of choosing swing trading as your strategy include:

1. It is hard to find that perfect market where a particular stock is going to end up trading between the resistance and the support levels. This can get even harder to predict when there is a strong downtrend or a strong uptrend that are at work.
2. Penny stocks can make it hard to time your buys the right way, especially when dealing with dilution on the stock that you purchased.

Technical Trading

Technical trading is a good option to go for when you are looking at all the points of your trading strategy. This one is going to use a Technical Analysis in order to help you find the right stocks that you would like to trade as well as helping you to set up your entry and then exit points to reduce losses if they would occur. Someone who picks to go with this kind of trading is going to use charts in order to examine the whole history of the stock, take the time to observe indicators that is going on, and then they will be able to identify the trends and patterns that are going on with the price.

There are a few different indicator groups that you can use in order to work with technical trading. Some of these include:

1. Strength indicators: these are the indicators that are going to compare your current price to that of its history. This helps to show how weak or strong the stock will be. The Relative Strength Indicator is the most common one to use with this. Often, it is shown at the top of your charts and it will indicate any overbought as well as oversold price conditions. Many times, this can be a tip for helping you to buy and sell at the right price for a stock.

2. Moving averages: these are known as MA's, and they are indicators that are going to be generated by averaging out the price levels over so much time. These can help you to see how often the movements of the stock are either below or above their averages. These are known as crossovers and can sometimes indicate breakdowns and breakouts as well, something that is important to a trader who is trying to pick out what stock they would like to work with.

3. Pattern analysis: this is the evaluation of your charts in order to identify price formations, such as shapes, that come up in history. Sometimes, you are able to see wedges, triangles, cups, handles, and more for the stock you want to work with. These formations can sometimes be used to see into the future and determine if there is going to be any downward or upward movement. They are often caused by market forces, but one showing up, whether it is natural or not, will affect the action of that stock.

4. Range analysis: this is where you are going to use a few different things together, such as the price range and the closing and opening prices in order to figure out where your resistance and support levels are. These can help you to figure out what the best purchases, as well as sell points, are and can tell you other information, such as the levels of a breakdown and breakout with the stock.

5. Gap analysis: this one is going to be done when you are able to find gaps in the charts you are looking at. A gap is going to be a spot that is inside the chart which will be caused by a price at the opening that is higher than what it was at the close the previous time period. The idea behind here is that these gaps are usually going to be filled so you

will be able to use this in order to figure out the buy prices since you know that the price will go back down to fill up this gap before it goes higher.

All of these options are going to need you to use analysis in order to figure out when to enter the market, how long to hold on to the penny stock, and when to let them go in order to make the biggest profit possible while limiting your losses. There are many benefits of using this kind of strategy including:

1. There are many people who are on the forums and the boards who will help you to learn how to use TA and will talk to you about how to identify these hot stocks.
2. Inside of penny stocks, these technical moves can be pretty strong. This is because TA is all there really is to help you to judge a stock and the way that the price will move.

Of course, while there are many people who will use this option to help them make decisions with their trading, there are a few cons that you will need to worry about. Some of these cons include:

1. Bashers and pumpers can make almost all charts look like they are negative or positive, in the hopes of luring investors without experience into doing the action that they want.
2. Without paying attention to some of the fundamentals, such as the news, a trade that looks good in this analysis could quickly turn around in just a few minutes and you could lose out.
3. Using a technical analysis can be hard. It is complex and hard for some people to understand how to use.

Scalping

One of the other strategies that you can use when working in penny stocks is known as scalping. This is when the investor is going to make several trades throughout the day in order to make some small profits on one of the stocks that really don't move during that day. The scalper is going to use the bid and ask spread to make this work. They will buy their shares at the big, or somewhere close to it, they can then turn around and make a small profit. This one is not going to make them a ton of money, but it is better than nothing if you plan it out right and the market isn't moving.

You are able to repeat this kind of profit a few times in order to increase your profits. While you may only make a few dollars on each trade, when you do hundreds of these, you can make a lot of money through the day. This is sometimes considered day trading but be aware that all day trading is not scalping. Sometimes, this strategy will do well, but you need to be careful because most stocks are not going to stay constant and you may end up with one that goes down in value through the day.

There are a few benefits that come from using the scalping method in your trading strategy. Some of these benefits include:

1. For the most part, your penny stocks are going to have a large spread, which helps to give you a good profit.
2. Penny stocks are sometimes going to trade sideways right after they finish with a big move or when they are trying to break through the resistance level.
3. When you purchase at the bid and then sell right away at the ask, you will still get the lowest price on your purchase and it reduces the risk when you sell as quickly as possible before things can change.

Of course, there are a few negatives that can come up from using the scalping process for your penny stocks. Some of the cons of going with this method include:

- Penny stocks can be difficult to do this with because of their anemic volume.
- This process is going to make you work against your

market makers, and this makes it difficult.

- Since penny stocks are high risk and this option is only going to give you a small amount of profit, it may not be the best. If you want to give it a try, it isn't bad, but some people don't think the risk is worth the reward.

All of these strategies have been used when it comes to working in penny stocks and it is important to figure out which method you would like to use for your needs. You can pick any of them and see some success, but you do need to be careful. You are not going to see the good results that you want if you are skipping all over the place and not sticking with a good strategy. Those who are the most successful with penny stocks, as well as with some of the other investment options are the ones who will pick out one strategy and stick with it. Consider some of the strategies that we talked about in this chapter and choose the one that works the best with your needs and will help you to make the biggest profit in penny stocks.

No matter what strategy you use, there are best practices that all experienced and successful traders observe. These are the keys that will help you succeed. These things are not just something that you read because their true essence is in doing, so be sure to apply them to your every trade. Here are the best trading practices that you should know:

Do your research

Do not simply focus on the penny stocks that you want to purchase. Keep in mind that the performance of stocks heavily depends upon the overall performance of the business. Therefore, you must also give attention to the company itself. How is the company doing in the market? Does it match up well against its competitors? Remember to research the penny stocks that you intend to purchase, as well as the company concerned.

The scope of research is, of course, a big task. This is one of the most important parts of trading. Also, find out the factors that affect a particular stock and understand them. Are these factors present at the current moment? Is there any chance that any of these influential factors appear in the future? If so, what are the consequences? The more research and knowledge that you have, the better is your chances of investing in the right penny stocks.

Only invest the money you can afford to lose

A very common piece of advice known to all gamblers is this: "Only play with the money you can afford to lose." This is common advice given to gamblers. Although trading penny stocks may not be considered gambling, especially if you do not rely on pure luck, it is still similar to gambling in the sense that there is always the possibility to lose your money. Do not use the money that you need for your child's enrolment or for paying the household bills, etc. Although there is no assurance that you will lose your money, you must only invest the money that you can afford to lose. The penny stock market is very volatile that it is hard to guarantee that you will make a profit.

Set a limit

It is sound advice, especially for beginners, to decide before making any trade on a limit on how long you will continue to hold on to a losing stock, as well as for a profitable one. The penny stock market is extremely volatile. Although you can expect for their value to increase and decrease almost randomly, it does not always mean that a stock whose price has just decreased will soon increase.

Part of the volatility of penny stocks is that a significant decrease in value can still be followed by another big drop. Therefore, in order to cut down your losses, it is important to set a limit on how long you would be willing to hold on to a losing stock. In the same way, you should know how long you will hold on to a winning stock. Again, even if a stock continuously experiences an increase in value, there is still the possibility that its price can just drop dramatically, almost without any warning.

Look for patterns

The movement of the prices of penny stocks can be said to be like random. The thing is, randomness creates patterns. And, if it is not random, then there is more possibility to find a pattern. If you can identify these patterns early, then you will be one step ahead. Just remember, though, that patterns are like trends; and in the world of penny stocks, they do not last for very long.

Observe the trends

Analyze the graphs and tables that show the performance of certain penny stocks. Do not just study their current record, but also check their past performance. This is a good way for you to know if the stocks are really doing well or not. Also, do not rely completely on the latest trends. Although the latest trends can show you the most recent performances of penny stocks, you must take note that trends often change. In fact, in the penny stock market, you will barely see a trend that will last for too long.

Know the latest news

If you are serious about trading penny stocks, then you should be updated on the latest news. The many factors that affect the prices of penny stocks are usually revealed on the news. Although the news would not state it directly, you should know that laws, businesses, economy, market behavior, and inflation, among others, can affect the prices of penny stocks. Take note, however, that although the news can give you valuable insights and information, what matters the most is still the actual prices of penny stocks.

Stay calm

Bad days do happen, and you may encounter a series of losing streaks despite doing some good research. During such a moment, or the moment when you first experience your first loss, stay calm. I repeat, stay calm. The penny stock market does not care about how you feel, so you must remain objective and focused. If you cannot control yourself, just quickly turn off your computer or mobile phone.

Do not be greedy

Especially for beginners, it is recommended that you stick to getting small yet regular profits. Many inexperienced traders lose their money not because of buying the wrong penny stocks, but because of keeping the stocks for too long. Do not underestimate the highly volatile nature of the penny stock market. Learn to sell, cash out, and enjoy your profit.

Keep your emotion under control

Do not be an emotional trader. Although it is good to feel passionate about trading penny stocks, do not let your passion blind your judgment. Never make any trade when under pressure and treat trading penny stocks as a business.

Make your own decision

Although it is advisable to read the opinions of "experts," it is wrong to let them dictate your investment decisions. Unfortunately, many of these so-called "experts" are hacks and frauds. They promote themselves as an expert even if their overall losses outweigh their profits. Of course, there are still a few real experts out there, but even the best traders still commit mistakes from time to time. After all, the process of developing your trading strategy is a life-long journey.

Instead of relying on expert advice, you should develop your own understanding of the penny stock market and make your own decisions. You can compare your decisions with the pieces of advice given by "experts" and see how well you match up. Of course, you also need to check the real outcome of a particular trade to see if you have made the right investment decision.

Do not chase after your losses

This is another advice given to gamblers. Unfortunately, although this advice is very common, many still fail to observe it. There are several ways to chase after your losses, but they all usually lead to the same unfortunate result. Usually, you chase after your losses by investing more right after you lose a trade. When you lose, you simply have this strong urge to get your money back. Another thing people do is by continuously holding on to losing stocks, thinking that once they sell them, they would no longer save their lost investment. In any way, you are on the losing side with just a little hope of getting your losses back. The bad thing here is that you gamble your whole funds for the sake of recovering a few losses. Therefore, the risk is really high.

A good way to avoid this is by learning to accept your losses. If certain penny stocks fail to meet your expectations, learn to accept your losses by selling them and starting over again. When you seriously engage in trading penny stocks, losing some investments is normal. After all, once you get lucky and hit truly profitable stocks, you will quickly recover all your losses and enjoy grand profits.

Stick to your strategy

During the execution process, you must do your best to stick to your planned strategy; otherwise, you will not be able to measure effectiveness, as well as its full potential. Of course, there are instances that you should abandon your strategy, especially if circumstances clearly show that continuing with your strategy will result in a total loss of investment.

Only invest in penny stocks that have a high volume

According to some "expert," you should only invest in stocks that trade at least a hundred thousand shares per day. This serves as a safeguard against the risk of being illiquid.
86

Pump your stocks

There is a reason why the pump and dump scheme still exists despite many people being aware of such a scheme: It works.

So, if you do not mind being a bit tricky, you can market yourself as an "expert" in trading penny stocks. You can put up a website and send out newsletters to your readers. You can then purchase cheap penny stocks, use your connections to gain interest in the stocks, and sell them at a premium price. If you are the type that can convince people to do what you want, then this may be an easy way for you to make money. However, if you are the type who cannot exercise a bit of trickery (which is a very good thing about you), then you can simply take advantage of people who pump and dump their stocks. How? Simply buy their penny stocks, preferably before they pump them or as early as possible while they pump their value. You can then wait for their price to increase, sell your penny stocks, and reap some profits.

Keep a journal

Writing a journal is not required, but it is very helpful. You do not have to be a professional writer to write a journal. What is important is for you to be honest about everything that you write.

There are many things that you can write in your journal. It is also good to write your goals and reasons for why you want to trade penny stocks. Also, write any lessons and mistakes that you have learned. It is your journal, so feel free to write about anything and everything about your trading adventure. A journal will allow you to think outside the box and be a smarter trader.

Take a break

Trading penny stocks have a gambling factor: It can be addicting. It is something that you can do for hours without being tired. You would feel more like playing than working.

However, when you engage in research, which is a must, that is the time where you will definitely feel that trading penny stocks involve serious work. Allow yourself to take a break from time to time. Remember that you will have better mental clarity if you give yourself a chance to take a rest.

Get the latest updates quickly

Successful traders get the latest news and respond quickly. The way to take advantage of the impact of the news on the prices of stocks is by making the appropriate trading actions just before others realize them. For example, when you see that your penny stocks will soon encounter a massive drop in value, sell them right away. Also, if possible, know the news before it is even released in the public. To increase the probability that certain stocks will increase in value, the stocks should also be effectively promoted. Therefore, it is helpful if you can join and be active in online groups and forums on penny stocks.

Focus on start-up companies

One of the best things about the penny stock market is that it is a place where you can find many start-up companies. Surely, a good number of these companies will do well. Unfortunately, some of them will perform badly and even get bankrupt. However, if you manage to get the stocks of the good start-up companies early on, you will find yourself in a winning position.

Therefore, you must exert the effort to research and analyze the different start-up companies that participate in the penny stock market. When analyzing a particular company, also measure how it matches up against its competitors in the market.

Growing companies have lots of space for improvements; and as their profits increase and they continue to expand, the prices of their penny stocks also increase.

Have fun

It is common advice that you should choose a job that you enjoy. In the same way, you should enjoy trading penny stocks. If you do not enjoy it, then maybe it is a signal that you should just invest somewhere else. Also, you can make better decisions when you are having fun.

Choose the right penny stocks

Always choose the right penny stocks to invest in. How do you know the right ones? Sufficient research. Never commence a trade without sufficient research. Take note that little research is not enough. Researches made without serious efforts are only as good as a mere toss of a coin. Also, the most profitable and attractive-looking stocks may not always be the right penny stocks to invest in. After all, no matter what the media says, the numbers on the penny stock market are what counts.

Be patient

Patience is important when you trade penny stocks. Do not hurry to make a buy order simply because you have funds in your account. Also, many times, to take advantage of the high volatility of penny stocks, you will have to wait for some time. Take note that every action that you make is essential. The stocks that you buy today are the stocks that you will soon sell. Be patient, wait for the proper timing, and act accordingly.

Use the high volatility to your advantage

Although many people shy away from penny stocks due to their high volatility, it is this volatile nature of penny stocks that make them a profitable investment. With high volatility, mastering the famous principle for making money is the key to profit: buy when the price is low, and sell when the price is high.

As a beginner, you may be a bit worried about getting started with penny stocks. These are going to take a different route compared to working with traditional stock market options, and sometimes, it is hard to find the information that you need about the company before making the investment that you want. With that being said, it is possible to be successful when using penny stocks. You just need to be careful with the decisions that you make in penny stocks and take your time to really see results. Some of the tips that you can follow when you get started with penny stocks to help you be successful include:

Ignore some of the success stories

When you first get started with penny stocks, you are going to get a lot of information and emails about the success stories of others who have done well with penny stocks. These are found in social media sites and in emails, but often, these are unusual circumstances or the information is all made up.

Instead of focusing on this, you need to look at the stocks on their own and see if they are going to work for you. Just ignore all of the success stories since most of these are going to be in order to get you to make a certain purchase. Do your research and learn about the market to determine which ones are the right ones for you.

Read through the disclaimers

If you are receiving a newsletter about the penny stocks, you need to be careful about the tips that you are reading. There is nothing wrong with picking out some of the stocks from these options, but you should be aware that most of them are sales tips and to give exposure to companies that, for the most part, are really bad and could end up making you lose a lot of money.

Most of the newsletters that you are going to pick won't give you the full story. The people who are writing them will do so in order to pump out the stock and they are not going to tell you the right time to sell the stocks. They will work hard to get you to purchase their stocks, and then, you never hear from them again. It is fine to read through some of these to get some information, but when the disclaimers state that these are written as a promotion for one company or another, you know that the tips are more of a sales pitch rather than as good advice.

Sell quickly

One of the allures that you will hear about with penny stocks is that you are able to get a huge return on investment, up to 30 percent, in just a short amount of time. If you want to make a return on investment like this with penny stocks, you will need to sell your stocks quickly after you purchase them. Unfortunately, instead of being happy with the 30 percent or so, people will get greedy and will look to make a huge return. Considering penny stocks are sometimes getting pumped out and the industry is volatile, you should be happy with what you get or you may lose out on a lot of money.

Be careful when listening to the company management

You need to be really careful about the people you are listening to the inside of penny stocks, even when it comes to company management of the stock that you are working with. These companies are trying to work in order to get the stocks up. When the stocks up, these companies are able to raise more money and it is more likely they will stay in business. In some instances, they may not even be companies, but basically, insiders who are trying to get rich.

In fact, most of the promotions that you will see come from the same group of people who will use different companies and press releases in order to get some hype up and make some extra money. They may have purchased the stocks at a lower price and now want to create a lot of buzzes to get you to make a purchase much higher than what they paid.

In between the people who are using a pump and dump to make money and the companies who are worried about going under and want to get you to agree with them to save them from failing, it is hard to know which penny stocks are safe. You need to think independent of the news and some of the promotions that you hear before picking out the stocks that you want to invest in. With some good research and being critical of things you hear, it is easier to pick out the penny stocks that are actually good and to make the money you want.

Focus on high volume

When you are getting started, it is best to only use stocks that have a minimum of 100,000 shares traded each day. If you go with a stock that is too low in volume, it is sometimes too hard to get yourself out of this issue. In addition, experts recommend that you pick out the stocks that are selling for over 50 cents a share. Going with stocks that are lower in price than this may seem appealing, but often, these aren't considered liquid enough to really play with. But if you pick out stocks that are getting more than 100,000 shares a day traded and they are over 50 cents for each share, you are going to have more luck getting them to sell nicely.

Pick the best stock out of the bunch

You should make sure that you pick out one of the best stocks that you can find, especially when you are a beginner in this industry. Some experts recommend that you find a stock that has really good earnings overall or one that has broken out of its average 52-week highs in volume. Some of these are easy to find, but the trick with these is that you want to find ones that have these highs, but not because of a pump and dump scheme. You want the highs to be because others are interested in the stock and the value is going up naturally, not because of some buzz that is created to inflate the price.

Never fall in love with just one stock

When it comes to the stock market and with penny stocks, you can't fall in love with one stock. When you decide that one stock, and only one, is the option that you will go with, you are going to end up failing. You won't look at the stock in an objective way and this can make it hard to stick with your guns and make sure that you are thinking about profit.

There are always going to be salespeople who can come to you with a great story about their company and will make you fall in love with their product. But your job is to look at something objectively to find out if it is actually going to make you the money that it promises. With some good research and hard work, you will be able to find the right options for your needs without falling prey to others who want your money.

Do your research

Before you get into any of the stocks, you need to make sure that you complete your research. There is not much information that is provided inside of the penny stocks, although there are a few companies that will provide this information to help you out. This means that you will need to get to work and do some research. Look up the company and learn a bit about them including some press releases and other news that surrounds them. You should take a look at the market overall and see where things are going. You can even look at the current stock and see its history to learn how things are going for the company.

When you finish the right research before making a decision, you will find that it is easier than ever to get the results that you want. You will be able to make informed decisions, rather than just jumping into the mix and hoping that it all works out for the best.

Keep your head

If you are new to penny stocks, you may find that it is easy to get really involved with the stocks. You may get too involved, feeling that you need to keep going when you are losing money and getting too upset, or too happy, when things aren't going the way that you want. It is important to look at all of this objectively and learn how to always keep your head and think critically, no matter what is going on in the market.

For those who lose their tempers quickly, those who have an addictive personality, or those who will have trouble with these almost gambling-like options, it is not a good idea to get into penny stocks. You need to be able to take control of the situation, no matter what happens, so that you can think critically and make decisions that will help you to make the most money possible with penny stocks.

When you are first getting started with penny stocks, you may be worried about how you will get to the top and start earning money with this kind of market. Follow some of these simple steps so that you can learn how to work with penny stocks and get them to work for you.

Chapter 7: 10 strategies to trade like a pro

- *"Have a long-term mindset"*. According to Warren Buffett, the shares once bought, are not to be sold. It is better to evaluate the industrial trends in the long term and then buy them, leaving aside the passengers' enthusiasm.

- *"When investing in real estate, know the area you are investing in"*. To start with, it is good that you put your focus on your area of residence or, if you live in a big city, even on your neighbourhood or on one that you know well. If you think to act on a field of action too large, you risk dispersing too much energy towards something that can present totally different solutions. Dedicate yourself only to residential buildings, apartments, or houses. The commercial ones, even if they can be very profitable, have other rules, and in general, greater difficulties. The same for the land: you can do big business, but it is not something suitable for those who start.

- *"Choose the right leverage and use it to your advantage"*. Real estate investments must be done with leverage. If you want to make an investment only with your money, then the essence of real estate investment is not clear to you. In fact, the concept of financial leverage allows you to invest with money that is not your, but to make money directly for you. Leverage an economic tool that allows you to get where you would not get only with your own strength. You can take out a mortgage (if you can afford it) or engage financial partners. It may seem strange to you but it is not at all: even the richest need partners and remember that a figure that seems almost unimaginable to you, it may be normal to somebody else.

- "*Verba volant, scripta manent*" the Latins used to say. So never make verbal agreements, even if it is a relative or a childhood friend. Consult a lawyer to have the templates of the documents to be used. Like everything, at first, it will seem difficult, but after a few times, you will become an expert in basic legal practices for the sale of real estate and you will be able to create documents in a very short time even by yourself.

- "*Consider shorter positions*". In the fixed income universe, a short duration approach is potentially able to reduce sensitivity to rising interest rates, while optimizing the returns/risk ration.

- "*Know your risk/reward ratio*". A higher return may be tempting, but you must be sure not to take too many risks in relation to the remuneration you would get. In bond markets, this means avoiding lengthening duration in a context of rising interest rates. Increasing investments in riskier assets may seem appropriate at the moment when the macroeconomic scenario is quite positive, but it could turn out to be a rather risky choice if the situation should change. For example, the yields offered by high yield debt, on average 3% in Europe and 5.5% in the United States, would not be sufficient to compensate investors if insolvencies passed from their current level of 2% to a more normal one of the 5%. Conversely, market areas with a good risk/return profile, with high-rated issuers offering attractive returns include emerging market debt, subordinated financial bonds, and hybrid corporate bonds. Aiming at long-term quality makes it possible to take on fair risks, helping to limit the impact of any negative macroeconomic event.

- "*Take the currency pairing into account*". Global investments exposed to currency risks. High yield bonds and emerging market funds, for example, are usually denominated in US dollars, but the underlying bonds they hold may be issued in another currency. Fund managers may choose to include currency risk in the overall portfolio risk as exchange rates fluctuate, or decide to contain this risk through currency hedging.

- *"Stay flexible, keep some cash aside"*. It is important to have the flexibility to underwrite and liquidate investments to seize the best opportunities. However, trades are expensive and can quickly erode earnings. This happens, above all, in the bond markets, given the relatively low levels of returns. The bid-ask spread is on average 30-40% of the yield, so an excess of trades erodes this margin and obviously reduces the total return. Even holding portfolios with structurally short duration, allowing short-term bonds to come to maturity naturally, can improve returns because you will effectively pay the bid-ask spread once.

- *"Build up your portfolio over time"*. If investing a small sum such as 5000 Euros will not allow you to live on that income, it can certainly represent an opportunity to make money. In addition, even if you have good economic availability, the ideal is always "to make it safe", starting investing from small figures and then fuel the investment over time.

- *"The past does not equal the future"*. The story is not indicative of how an investment will result in the future and investors should always try to weigh the potential risks associated with a particular investment, as well as its possible returns.

Chapter 8: Understanding the vocabulary

Who wants to invest or play on the stock exchange cannot consider or know some terms which are basic for their trading actions? Some precautions must be taken into consideration:

- Read, constantly and daily, newspapers of an economic nature; this will mainly serve those who are not very familiar with the terminology used and consequently do not know the meaning of Actions, Bots, BTPs, Dow Jones, NASDAQ, Nikkei etc.
- Watch economic news regularly in such a way as to familiarize yourself and learn how to pronounce the most used terms;
- Document yourself through books, forums, and online sites, this will greatly facilitate understanding and will also serve as personal cultural baggage. In this way, you can increase your knowledge and take your first steps in the world of economics.

A first term to know is certainly the word *share*, which is the cardinal element of the companies, which represents in all respects a share of the social capital of a company. The shares can be divided mainly into 3 categories:

- Ordinary shares: according to which the holder can express his right to vote;
- Savings Shares: there is no possibility to cast a vote but give a greater dividend than previous shares;
- Preference Shares: guarantee "a greater privilege" in the allocation of profits and voting power in extraordinary shareholders' meetings.

During your investing journey, you will find yourself in contact with other important terms you should know. Some of the most popular ones are:

- BOTs, ordinary treasury bonds: they are issued in the short term and provide for a minimum subscription amount, which will be around €1,000 and a return is given by the difference between the repayment value and the purchase value;
- BTPs, multi-year Treasury bills: issued in the medium and long term, providing a fixed rate and a six-monthly coupon as a periodic earnings prospect for the security;
- CCT, Treasury credit certificates: issued in the medium and long term, and like the previous ones, these also provide for a six-monthly coupon with the addition of a yield indexed to that of the BOT;
- CTZ, zero coupon Treasury certificates: these provide for fixed-rate securities, without a six-monthly coupon and have a variable maturity between 18 or 24 months.
- Dow Jones Index of the American stock exchange that contains the thirty most important titles;
- NASDAQ, always referring to the American stock exchange and which contains the titles with high technological content;
- Nikkei, from the Japanese stock exchange. Deals with the securities of the Japanese market;
- FTSE MIB, Financial Times Stock Exchange of Milan, inherent in the Italian stock exchange and concerns an average of the main Italian high capitalization securities;
- FTSE America Mid Cap, again the American stock exchange, including the securities of mid-cap companies;
- FTSE America Small Cap includes the small capitalization companies of the American stock exchange;
- MIB 30, contains the main American securities, and in particular, the first 30 American companies;
- MIBTEL, an index that contains a weighted average of all the most important American titles.

Before getting started, it is important to learn the basic terms and how they are used by the experts. In this chapter, you will find a simplified dictionary with the most popular words related to the investing niche.

Stock market

The stock market is the digital place where the largest number of transactions involving the shares, i.e. the shares of corporate capital, takes place.

In Italy, for example, the stock market is called MTA - Electronic Stock Market - and it should be noted that it does not coincide with the famous "Borsa di Piazza Affari" but represents one of the most important segments.

In fact, at Piazza Affari, different types of financial instruments are traded, and the market is divided according to the type of contracts traded in:

- MTA, the electronic stock market;
- SEDEX, the segment in which instruments such as covered warrants and certificates are traded;
- MOT, the electronic bond market in which bonds like (with the exception of those convertible into shares), government bonds, Eurobonds, and ABS, i.e. securities deriving from the security of loans are traded;
- TAH, After hours, the electronic market in which it is possible to negotiate after the closing of the Exchange, but only for the instruments of the MTA (shares) and the SEDEX (covered warrants and certificates);
- ETF plus, the electronic market in which UCITS units or shares are traded (SGRs and Sicavs);
- IDEM, the market for derivative instruments (futures and option contracts on currencies, interest rates, and financial instruments). Exceptions are forwarders that are derivative contracts traded on OTC markets, over the counter, which is not regulated.

Market capitalization

The stock market is also divided into sections by the capitalization threshold.

What, however, is the market capitalization?

The size of a listed company is measured in capitalization, that is, the value given by the number of shares available for that company multiplied by their market price.

The sections in which common markets are divided are:

- Blue chip, where the shares of the 40 largest companies are traded (over 1000 million Euros);
- Mid Cap, where the securities of the 60 listed companies with high capitalization are traded but which do not fall among the Blue chips;
- Small Cap, where the shares of companies that do not fall between the Blue chips or the Mid Cap are bought or sold;
- Micro Cap, for companies that do not fall within the minimum liquidity criteria necessary for the other segments;
- Star, for companies with a capitalization of between 40 and 1,000 million Euro, but with high transparency, governance, and liquidity requirements;
- MTA International where the shares of companies listed on EU exchanges is traded.

Stocks

The stocks are portions in the shared capital of companies, incorporated in joint-stock companies. The two main types of stocks are:

- Ordinary Stocks are those held by the shareholders of a company. They hold voting rights in corporate assemblies and profits deriving from dividends and capital gains;

- Savings Stocks, shares of this type do not have voting rights, but they guarantee patrimonial privileges such as dividends, i.e. the distribution of profits. They are mainly intended for small investors.

Stock value

Each share of each company is traded or bought or sold on a price basis: the market value. This price evolves continuously on the basis of the number and the sign of the contracts concluded.

For example, if you read that the Enel stock is up today, it means that many investors are buying Enel shares.

For the classical laws of economic demand and supply, if the demand rises, the price also rises. At the end of the day, when the session is officially closed, the official price of the Enel share will be obtained in this case, by the result of all the fluctuations that the value of the stock suffered during the session based on the number of exchanges it is traded on.

Chapter 9: How to Select the Best Stock to Invest In

What drives an investor to buy the shares of a company at that particular moment? As we have already said, the formation of share prices is a dynamic process like any other commodity market.

The value of a company stock affects:

- Corporate performance (the state of health of the company, the size of its assets, future growth prospects, ownership structures, and extraordinary finance transactions such as acquisitions, mergers and demergers): the improvement in performance is matched by an increase in price and investor's propensity to buy those shares; vice versa, the opposite happens, that is, depreciation. Who owns those shares will sell them, increase the bid, and drop the price in question;
- Performance of the sector, or the performance at the same time as other companies belonging to the same sector, also on other global stock exchanges;
- Macro or foreign policy data directly or indirectly relevant to a company: positive news generates purchases and appreciation, negative news push sales and the depreciation of the stock;
- news or rumours about the company, such as the discovery of new deposits for companies in the oil sector, or the registration of a new patent for a company in the pharmaceutical sector or news about possible mergers, joint ventures, or acquisitions.

CFD

This is a key point that actually explains why there is much less bureaucracy for forex trading than for buying and selling bank

104

shares. CFDs (Contract for Difference) are contracts for differences that follow the performance of a given underlying (share, currency, index, etc.) and that can be exchanged, that is, bought or sold. CFDs differ from shares because they are not co-owned by a company, and therefore, do not give voting rights to those holding them. However, CFDs offer the same economic benefits as equities, such as profits, dividends, and splits.

In even more technical terms, the CFD exchanges the difference in value between the opening price of certain underlying security (e.g. share) and its closing price. Following this mechanism, the trader who negotiates CFDs:

- Gets a positive result if it buys before the underlying goes up
- Gets a negative result if it sells before the underlying goes down

The mechanism is very simple, and we are sure that it is already clear. We need to buy if we think that a stock is close to the upside. We need to sell it if we think that a stock is close to the downside. CFDs follow the values of the underlying assets, so you can get positive results just like shareholders, but playing at home from the comfort of your home.

Is it better to invest in shares of 10 companies belonging to different sectors or invest in shares of 10 companies belonging to the same sector?

Another very important rule to follow when investing in online trading is to diversify your investment portfolio. Diversifying simply means investing in various equity securities, possibly from companies that operate in different sectors and markets. The reason for this choice is very simple: if you invest in securities belonging to different sectors, you can better mitigate the risk associated with the investments made.

In other words, in the event that a part of shares causes me a loss, I can amortize this loss thanks to the gains made with other stocks. This is why we must never invest all of our capital on the shares of a single company: if the value of the shares of that company falls, the loss that we will suffer will be very large. But if we have only invested a portion of my capital on these securities, my loss will be less, and at the same time, I will be able to make the remaining capital invested in other securities.

On the other hand, as regards the idea of investing in shares in the same sector, the reasoning is just bad. Investing in different stocks, but the entire same financial sector (such as banking, or automotive, or services, etc.), can expose you to major risks. Just to give an example, the American banking sector in 2019 definitely had the worst performance among all the securities listed on the Italian Stock Exchange. The reason is simple: our banks have many "impaired loans", i.e. loans that are no longer able to collect.

The bad performance of the banking sector has led to the loss of many equity securities linked to banks and the insurance sector. A trader who had only invested in shares in this sector would have ended 2019 with many losses, relating to all of his shares. But if you choose a couple of titles in different sectors, the possibility of running into this risk decreases.

Here is a summary of two principles you need to remember when you decide to invest in the stock market:

- Avoid investing money only on a single stock;
- Avoid investing in equity securities belonging only to a specific sector listed on the stock exchange.

Chapter 10: Mistakes You Have To Avoid

When you reach an intermediate level, there are certain mistakes that you risk to make. Here are some of the most famous ones and how to avoid them.

Number 1

The mistake: Confusing a nominal yield with a real yield. To think that it is easy to have a return above the average and that it is mediocre to invest in order to aim at the average market yield.
What you need to know: The average return is provided by economic growth. To have an excess return, it is necessary that someone else in the market has a sub-reward.
A good answer to the error: Invest in index funds or ETF funds to have healthy long-term returns. Add liquidity or bonds to adjust the risk/return ratio.

Number 2

The mistake: Buy only shares of well-managed companies.
What you need to know: The stock is not the company! The difference lies in the price you pay for the share.
A good answer to the error: Buy investment instruments that diversify widely, such as ETFs or index funds

Number 3

The mistake: To think that if a financial instrument has given good returns in the past, it is more likely that it will continue to do so in the future. Pay management fees based on past returns.
What you need to know: The financial markets are completely unpredictable. Every prediction on them has a probability of realizing (or not to be realized) oscillating between 40 and

60%

A good answer to the error: Do not pay commissions for active management based on past returns. Investing in the main categories of investments (stocks, bonds, real estate, liquid assets, and alternative instruments) based on your financial objectives, tolerance, and propensity for financial risk.

Number 4

The mistake: Making decisions on individual financial instruments and not from the perspective of the portfolio as a whole.

What you need to know: The risk characteristics of the portfolio complex are largely predictable.

A good answer to the error: Pay attention to a good diversification of the portfolio complex that combines with the right dose of risk based on your objectives and possibilities.

Number 5

The mistake: To think that commissions, technical costs, and taxation are not important.

What you need to know: The management of savings in America costs an average of 3% per year. In the long run, this cost has a dramatic impact on the actual compound return.

A good answer to the error: Use simple securities for the bond component of the portfolio, ETF, or funds indexed to low management fees for the equity part.

Number 6

The mistake: Having all the savings in bank accounts or monetary instruments.

What you need to know: Financial markets pay a non-diversifiable "risk premium"

A good answer to the error: Having a well-diversified portfolio allows you to have additional income to the one deriving from your job.

Number 7

The mistake: To panic when things go wrong and be greedy when things go well

What you need to know: Future performance expectations have very little relationship to past returns.

A good answer to the error: Base the composition of the financial portfolio on the long-term expected risk/return ratio.

Number 8

The mistake: Never make changes to the composition of the portfolio even when your assets, due to markets or personal situations, have changed.

What you need to know: Some market fluctuations can generate non-recoverable losses with a normal financial market trend. The right ratio between risk/return is strongly influenced also by the consistency of the assets.

A good answer to the error: Check carefully the maximum bearable loss (in absolute value) on the basis of its assets and make the relevant adjustments in the investment components to comply with this risk constraint.

Number 9

The mistake: Spend a lot of time with newspapers, TV, and financial websites.

What you need to know: The non-diversifiable risk, the decrease in costs and taxes maintain their value even when they are used by everyone, the ideas for having extra-financial returns.

A good answer to the error: Do not try to buy the "right" stock or enter and exit at the "right time". Only liars can do it.

Number 10

The mistake: Relying on consultants who are good at moving the portfolio on the basis of unlikely forecasts of future market movements or paying high commissions for unproductive management of mutual funds or asset management.

What you need to know: The vast majority of financial services are structured in such a way as to produce powerful conflicts of interest between the client and the intermediaries. Since the client is the weaker party because it has less knowledge, these conflicts of interest translate into completely unproductive costs.

A good answer to the error: Consider the possibility of relying on independent financial planners paid only to parcels and
. money managers who keep commission levels very low and emphasize financial risk management rather than returns.

Markets in recent times have not only become more complex, but also more volatile.

In simple words, the risk is increased. Economic factors, central bank interventions, negative rates, low inflation, and algorithms are changing the equity, currency, and commodity markets.

It seems that you no longer look at the fundamentals, but you buy the title of the moment and the one that presents a lower risk (or, to say it better, people think it presents a lower risk).

In such difficult markets, small investors who invest in the stock market do not have an easy life. But this does not mean that they have to abandon the shares: with hard work and perseverance, everyone can become a skilled investor.

To help you start your journey, we have collected 15 of the most common mistakes beginner investors make. If you are able to avoid them, you will be one step ahead of the competition.

Relying on Emotions

Most people lose on the stock market because they cannot manage their emotions.

It is proven that small savers buy in the upward phase of the markets, and panic sells at the first sign of decrease. Then what happens is that the market recovers and they are now out.

This happens because of the poor financial education of the average American investor.

He, who does not know how to assess the risk and the diversification, cannot select the securities to put in the portfolio. He does not know how to calculate the average value of an asset. He does not even know how to use a spreadsheet to calculate the volatility of a stock. And, it is precisely the lack of ability to manage the risk that will make him resort to bad decisions which will ultimately result in a loss.

Speculating, Not Investing

Another mistake that many often make is to confuse speculating with investing.

If you invest for the very short term, you increase the risk, and it is not a question of investment but of speculation. Knowing how to define investment speculation is essential.

Before entering a title, you must define your time horizon and consider where to put the stop loss. One classical example of speculation is "binary options." They are often promoted as an investment, but they are really not. For those who do not know what they are, binary options are bets placed on the price of an asset in the next 30 seconds. Yes, you read that right. Seriously, stay away from them.

Investing without Planning

On the stock market, invested capital should not be necessary for daily life. Before investing, plan these goals. Someone invests because he wants to buy a bigger house in the future. Others may invest for when they retire, but also for a holiday. There are those who do it for their children.

The real question is... "Why are you investing?"

Thinking to Be Able to Predict the Future

What do Warren Buffet from Omaha and life coach Tony

Robbins have in common? Both agree on the big risk that comes when our money is at stake.

During an interview with CNBC, Tony Robbins warned against a big mistake that is committed when it comes to investing for the future, which is, trying to predict the ups and downs of the market.

No one can predict the future, says Robbins, and legendary investors like billionaire Warren Buffett and the founder of the titanic hedge fund Bridgewater Associates, Ray Dalio, tend to agree.

"Your plan for the future cannot be based on trying to time the market because you're going the wrong way."

Instead of buying and selling shares based on how small the change, Robbins suggests thinking long-term.

"You cannot afford to try and time the market. What we must do is study the long-term elements, and have a diversification plan that protects when we are wrong."

Buffett is also an important supporter of this type of strategy called "buy and hold," so much so that he wagered that the S & P 500 stock index would surpass hedge funds (which actively change investments). Now, it seems that most likely he will win that bet, which will bring him an extra $2 million in prize money.

Robbins also relies on the advice of Dalio, who founded the largest hedge fund in the world, Bridgewater Associates, which has difficulty identifying the right times to get in and out of investments. So, for Robbins, the best idea remains to look long-term, and both he and Buffett suggest that they consider investing in low-cost index funds as the best thing to do.

Not Paying Attention to Costs

We have said it in all languages: costs can kill you financially.

Investing $15,000 for 30 years can result in $106,000 capital if made with an ETF or a low-cost mutual fund, and $67,000 if it is carried out with a mutual fund that has 2% of TER. See it for yourself.

Realistically, saving costs is the only true "free money" that you can get as an investor. Financial products with high commissions are more often than not skylarks; just think of how overestimated Alfa management's idea is.

Changing the Duration of the Investment "On the Go"

It usually works like this: you have chosen a portfolio assuming a certain duration of the investment, then the market "coughs," an instrument within the portfolio loses 5-6%, you read some negative opinions about it, start to shake like a rabbit, and eventually sell. This change of time horizon does monstrous damages. It normally makes you lose about half of the gains. Solution: invest a little at a time and do not think about it anymore.

Not Diversifying

Diversification is useless only if you are able to predict the future and know what the best investment will be. If instead (as a normal human being) you do not have paranormal divinatory skills, you should diversify your portfolio a little without exaggerating (more on that later).

Doing Everything Your Broker Says

If the bank, the promoter, or the broker pushes a product, run to check the costs. In 9 out of 10 cases, it is the most convenient product for them and, as you can guess, the most expensive for you.

Not Reading Prospectuses and Contracts Well

By law, intermediaries are forced to write everything they do in a "contract" type of document. Often times, they will do it with that legal language that sends you into narcosis already in the second line. Hence, you have to read everything if you do not want bad surprises. Remember that you are responsible for your money and should not put the blame on others.

Buying Unit-linked (and Index-linked) Policies

These policies are among the less transparent financial products that can be found and are padded with high commissions in favor of those who sell them. The seller will tell you a lot of nice stories about the capital guarantee.

With a unit-linked (or index-linked) policy, nine out of 10 chances, you will have an expensive product with severe penalties in case of early disinvestment and, after 10 or 20 years of payments, you will typically be rewarded with a disappointing performance (but, if you can console yourself, you will have made the man who sold it to you very happy).

Buying Bonds from Your Bank

Bank bonds usually make less of a BTP of the same maturity, because they bear implicit charges, like costs, for example. Then, they are, on average, riskier and less liquid. This is even more true for subordinated bank bonds, whose holders, with the recent entry into force of the bail-in, are likely to be called to put their hands in the portfolio in the event of the issuer's default. Before buying these bonds, study them carefully, compare them with a governmental or supranational title (like

BEI, BIS, etc.), and only then decide.

Believing to Get Rich with Online Trading

The colorful world of online trading is teeming with gurus to convince you that you will become rich, thanks to their fabulous courses or their financial market forecasting site. Know that succeeding with trading is very difficult: in the vast majority of cases, you will end up losing money and time. Learn to save and invest, not to trade.

Listening to Economists, Politicians, and Mass Media

The noise in the ears distracts: eliminate it. So here is, for you and only for you, our personal list of noises that you have to get rid of.

- **Economists.** Think about how little they have put us right in the story: for example, in 2009, they did not recognize the worst crisis since the Great Depression of 1929 in spite of a myriad of signals, and above all, the fact that the recession was already under its way.

- **Politicians.** Except for rare exceptions, the events of any Parliament are lively, full of funny and quarrelsome characters that combine all the colors, going from crisis to sudden solutions, and then plunge again into tragic crises: perfect plots for journalistic-television sagas. Generally, the impact on the financial markets of all this is low.

  For example, despite the ups and downs of Italian politics, the spread has continued on its way, indifferent to everything but the ECB. Going on historical facts of weight, think that after the Japanese attack on Pearl Harbor in 1941 (which dragged the US into World War II), the stock index Dow Jones only lost 6% (and in the following 12 months it gained 2,20%).

- **Mass media:** newspapers, television. They bombard you with a continuous stream of news and data (often superficially explained) which lead you to deviate from your investment path (see point 2). Every day, some economic data comes out: sometimes they improve, sometimes they get worse, but, in the immediate future, they rarely impact on your investments. Just to say, during the last recession in the Eurozone (which began in March 2012 and ended in June 2013), Eurozone stock markets have gained about 13%. So, you focus on a few important things: check your wallet regularly, follow the right source of information, but do not be paranoid about the news.

Wanting to Become Successful Overnight

Do not be the investor who wants immediate success and who loses patience for daily highs and lows. Wanting quick results is certainly an example of how not to invest your savings if you want to succeed.

Investing successfully is a bit like taking care of a vegetable garden. Plants grow slowly, with the first few years bearing little fruits, but then start to grow faster. In general, it is foolish to expect significant results in a few weeks, months, or even in a few years. Remember that you do not want to get rich fast, you want to get rich for sure.

Not Taking Profits

It may seem strange, but there are lots of investors that never take out their profits. This is detrimental since they never enjoy the money they earned with investing. It is like getting a gym subscription, but never going to the gym: it is useless and does not bring back to the practice.

The most successful investors always take out profits from time to time. Obviously, we are talking about calculated decisions and planned moves. However, the gold nugget here is the fact that if you do not have the money in your bank account, you cannot actually use it. It may sound silly, but it is a fact that most beginners tend to forget.

Chapter 11: Lessons You Have To Know To Be a Successful Trader

Because of the continuous ups and downs that have involved international stock exchanges in recent months, many have begun to ask themselves the fateful question: "Is investing in shares still the best strategy to multiply my savings?".

The financial markets, in general, can be an extraordinary opportunity: not only stocks but also cryptocurrencies or forex can give great satisfaction even if, however, it is necessary to have preparation before going into rash choices.

In this chapter, we will go deep into the subject and discover the 31 golden lessons that every investor should know before entering the stock market.

1. Easy money is like Santa Claus: it does not exist!

Who promises to quintuple your assets without sweating is not more than a seller of smoke: investing in the stock market is not a joke, and to achieve the investment goals, you have set yourself to avoid risky securities, focusing on something more stable, lasting, and profitable. In the recipe for success, in addition to a serious knowledge of the stock markets, there is also the sentimental component (for those investing, there is no room for panic but a lot of patience) and even a bit of luck.

2. Gold and cash do not give interest

Everyone knows that cash does not disappear, but after the bizarre maneuverers of the European Central Bank (which brought negative returns on the single currency), we can even be more certain that investing in cash does not create any interest. The dream of all is to be able to accumulate that amount of money enough to enjoy a quiet retirement, but the closer it gets to the time x, the more the small investor tends to panic. Hence, the reckless choices to invest in cash or in commodities, such as gold which, although, it proves to be more stable than fiat, cannot hold the same value forever. Just think that in the last luster, the value of the most precious metal fell by 34.8%.

3. The ingredients for a winning strategy

One of the main factors of success on the stock exchange is sentiment: patience, foresight, and prudence are the three basic ingredients of winning strategies; but, it is also true that a little risk never hurts.

If the money we have invested on a certain stock does not return, you should look around and find some slightly riskier but at least profitable activity, with the hope that an important injection of money into the markets can restart the economy by stimulating productivity and development.

4. Establish investment goals

Before starting to invest then embark on a challenging and long path, you must have a clear mind on where you want to go. It depends on personal aspirations, on the trust that one has for himself, and on many other factors. However, the main choice is between protecting capital and making it grow. Under certain conditions, the stock exchange also lends itself to a thoughtful approach. Who wants to start establishing concrete objectives such as buying a good or a service? In any case, the rule is always the same: to understand where you want to arrive.

5. Establish the degree of risk tolerance

This is probably the most important phase. The stock market is, in fact, extremely varied and allows numerous approaches, from the prudent and static to the dynamic and courageous.

This is why it is always good to establish one's degree of tolerance. Based on this decision, further choices will be made until the real investment is realized. Investor profiles depend on personal characteristics and their economic situation. If you are a simple worker, do not sail in gold and, maybe, those who invest are the savings of a lifetime; it is good to give up any speculative ambitions. The degree of tolerance determines the risk that you intend to run and the strategy that will be adopted later.

6. Studying

The information issue should not be forgotten. The stock market is complex and structurally risky, so we need to be cautious. The risk is to lose capital in a short period of time. Therefore, it is necessary to undertake a training course that confers at least the theoretical tools. The topic of the study should consist of both the investment modalities - how it is invested in the concrete - and the economic environment in general.

As for the sources, including paper texts, successful books, and the internet, you are spoiled with choices.

The study activity, however, never abandons the investor, even when he has become an expert. Pressing is the need to update continuously but also to inquire about everything that gravitates around the securities in the portfolio.

7. Choose the long-term

Investing in the stock market should not be an activity of a few months or even a few years; it must be a continuous activity. It is only through patience and perseverance that it is possible to make substantial profits. This means that you need to build a long-term version, which looks at least for the next five years (even if ten are more suitable). This means that it is good not to give in to the temptation to sell the securities as soon as the prices start to fall.

8. Monitoring

If you opt for a long-term vision, as you should, then it is essential to monitor the status of your investment. Not everyone knows that control and monitoring start before the investment itself. In particular, it is necessary to establish a benchmark, i.e., a yardstick by means of which, it is possible to really understand whether we are on the right path or not. Finally, it is good to make a periodic comparison between the expected results and the real ones. In the beginning, there is a strong temptation to abandon oneself to discouragement, also because the results tend to arrive farther with time.

A general consideration can be made on the segment within which to operate. In fact, everything depends on risk tolerance. If this is very low, you should address those segments that, by their nature, do not suffer from the crisis. The reference is to those goods whose consumption is practically mandatory. For example, a food and pharmaceuticals. Investing in pharmaceutical companies will not make you rich but is a very useful asset to protect capital. Strangely enough, but up to a certain point, the high-tech segment (e.g., mobile phones, social networks, etc.) also plays a similar role.

Investing in the stock market can be a business that can increase its capital. In addition to technical knowledge, we need some moral skills: patience, perseverance, lucidity, and foresight. All qualities that must be cultivated and that can make the difference. Vice versa, will never give good fruits and approach based on imprudence on haste from the frenzy of profit.

9. Use the leverage

What, unfortunately, many traders do not consider is investing in the stock market or trading online using leverage. To invest in the stock market with little money, it is necessary to deepen the study of this tool, which will allow us to expose our capital to a huge risk. We recommend the use of leverage only on a reduced capital, carried out concurrently also with a rationalized use of stop loss and take profit. In addition, you must always have your budget under control using careful Money Management. Finally, before investing in the stock market, you need to study the markets and all the financial instruments on which you want to invest in.

10. You do not need to be a finance guru to invest in the stock market!

Obviously, we are not telling you that the market should not be studied or that there must be a basis for training. Who applies himself and follows the markets, deepening the subject, will always know more than others.

So, we always recommend following the training path of your broker, which will allow you not to take missteps throughout the investment process. When taking advantage of the online trading demo platforms, it is possible to simulate the investment and understand where mistakes are made and avoid them when investing with a real account.

11. Use only trusty brokers

We believe that the stock market is not a market for everyone but for a few! Above all, we cannot recommend the stock exchange, for the investments on the stock exchange to those subjects are not inclined to study at least the basic training. In this case, it is better to let go of one's own, as it is not possible to rely only on luck.

Our advice is to stay away if you do not have and do not want to learn specific skills. If you do not have a basic education, all the savings you decide to invest will be lost in less than a month. On the contrary, instead, we recommend investing in the stock market with online trading and regulated brokers. It is because by being regulated and being subjected to strict controls, they do not put capital at risk, and the broker will provide you with a fair and complete formation. Below, you will find a complete list of regulated and authorized brokers to invest with.

12. Learn technical analysis

Technical analysis is the study of price trends with the use of graphs. The interest of a technical analyst is to look for the graphics configurations that are drawn by price movements. The market trend is evaluated to understand possible future price movements.

The pure technical analysis is not based on any fundamental of the underlying activity but applies a series of technical tools drawn on the chart in order to allow for future courses.

On the chart, price movements are usually represented by bars or candles, allowing price analysis in a certain period called "time frame."

On a candle, the body or the central part represents the difference between opening and closing in a given period. The shadows, i.e., the top and bottom segments, represent the difference between the maximum and the minimum of the period considered and the opening or closing of the candle.

We can have monthly, daily, 1 hour, 5 minutes, or even shorter candles.

The different colors of the candles indicate a rise or fall in the period. Usually, a green candle represents a rise in prices, which means that the closing price of the candle is higher than the opening one, while the red candle represents a drop.

The levels of the chart where prices find an obstacle are called "the levels of support or resistance." A "support" is the level at which a bearish price halts its downfall and potentially "rebounds" up again. The most significant support is repeatedly tested and becomes the level of support from a technical point of view. The "resistance" is the opposite of the support. It is the level at which a rising price finds an obstacle to rise further and, instead, shows a decline. Even a resistance tested several times takes on higher strategic importance.

When prices determine an important level of support but then violate it downwards, this level of support becomes an important area of resistance. The same goes for resistance that, if violated on the upside, turns into a significant level of support.

There are so many indicators used by technical analysts to try and predict the next price movements. One of the most used indicators is the "simple moving average," which is calculated on a certain amount of price data and is mobile because it moves from period to period.

Given an average of a certain time frame, the most recent data is added each time, eliminating the last data in the series from the calculation. The moving average can be used as a support or dynamic resistance. The most used periods on the daily chart for the moving average are 50, 100, and 200. If prices show a major uptrend, the moving average will be an important medium/short-term support inversely. If prices show a bearish trend, the average mobile will be significant dynamic resistance.

13. Learn fundamental analysis

Unlike the previous one, it is based on the study of the company and its reference market.
In practice, it is based on balance sheet data, on management's ability, and credibility on trends in the specific sector in which the company operates. In this case, one must also consider:
- value investing
- growth investing
- investment

All traders have a different investing style. Every trader has his own investment techniques, and each has his own particular techniques, as well as his particular tricks and his particular "secrets."

Nevertheless, do not be fooled by the strange idea of being able to learn how to invest by reading articles on the internet; this is impossible. You can find excellent advice but not the magic formula. At most, you could clear your mind and give yourself a general orientation, but to get serious, you need longer and more in-depth things.

14. Analyze the state of the market

Closely connected to the concept of technical analysis and fundamental analysis is the concept of analysis of the general market. It does not matter whether you are a professional investor or a beginner; this will be the most difficult step you need to understand.

In practice, it is pure art applied to scientific instruments. You must first understand and analyze the market for the sole purpose of formulating a plausible development scenario. This also means accumulating an enormous amount of data and statistics regarding the performance of the securities and developing the "sensitivity" necessary to choose the truly relevant ones.

If you put this into practice, you will also understand why many investors buy the shares of a particular company and not of another one.

At the same time, we always advise you to observe the products you have at home. Although this element may seem unusual, it is very important to understand that you have direct knowledge of many products and not others. In practice, it will allow you to perform a quick and intuitive analysis of the financial performance of the manufacturing companies, comparing them with those of their competitors.

Before investing, you must reflect on the products examined. For example, try to imagine the economic conditions for which you might decide to stop buying that particular stock. This is a great exercise to get a feeling of what an average person needs and treats as "important."

15. Create an investment plan

You have to create an investment plan. To do that, you must

fully understand why you want to invest.

You must know how much you can invest in and how much you want to invest in achieving your goals. You must also have clear ideas about what your goals are. To do this, you could always use an Excel sheet or even a special tool to calculate how much you will have to spend to achieve your goals.

Based on the income, know what you can afford to invest then calculate the type of investment. You cannot claim to want to get $10,000 from an investment if what you can afford to invest in trading online, or on the stock exchange, or even in other systems does not exceed 1000 Euros. Everything must be proportionate; start small and build it up over time.

16. Understand Asset Location

Asset Location is defined as the distribution of liquidity in the various investment instruments available and should vary depending on the stage of life in which you are.

This means that if you are young, the percentage of your investment portfolio relative to the shares will have to be higher. On the contrary, if you have a solid and well-paid career, your job is like an obligation! You can use it in order to guarantee long-term income.
In this way, you can allocate most of your financial portfolio in shares.

At the same time, you have to understand that if you have a job whose remuneration is not predictable, as in the case where you are self-employed, then you have to allocate most of your financial portfolio in more stable products. In this case, it is better to invest in bonds, perhaps government bonds, and not in shares.

At the same time, however, you must consider that the actions allow faster growth of your invested assets, but as such, entails a greater risk.

17. Study the financial risk

Another element to take into consideration when choosing to invest in a stock exchange is a financial risk. We could define it as the risk linked to the fact that investment can go wrong.

This also assumes that the yield is lower than expected or may even go "red." So, be careful not to underestimate this element. On the other hand, it is an element that is not easy to understand and accept. At the same time, it is not infrequent, and it is due to different dimensions that it is always good to know.

The financial risk has, in fact, different facets. In practice, it could be of a different nature:

- **Specific:** linked to the performance of the single instrument we purchased
- **Systematic:** linked to the oscillation of the financial market of the manager; linked to the skills of those who manage yours
- **Money-related:** be it an investment fund manager, a financial planner, or consultant to whom you have been entrusted
- **Market timing:** the possibility of making mistakes when entering and/or leaving the market
- **Liquidity:** the possibility of having to sell a stock that has a little market (it is called a little liquid title) and to have a low price
- **Currency:** When buying security denominated in foreign currency, the yield will also depend on the ratio between the currency and the euro.

Analyzed according to these elements, financial risk is a bit more complex than the simple possibility that things go wrong. Understanding it and knowing how to manage these different risks can, therefore, shift the odds that things are going well in our favor.

18. Analyze and discover your risk tolerance

Another important element even before starting to invest in the stock market is to analyze one's risk appetite. All financial instruments are characterized by a different risk. For example, the price of stock varies over time more than that of a bond. Unfortunately, this should not be considered a reductive element. The risk is much higher than it might seem at first.

In analyzing a long-term time horizon and considering an investment in US stocks that have historically made very good and, therefore, considering them as a safe investment, we must always consider the risk that we could incur the complete loss of capital invested for a joke of the market that you did not foresee. So, you must also consider these factors.

Here, it is better to consider and analyze a more ambitious investment look. This means considering the investment portfolio and not a single instrument. To date, there are different ways to make different instruments coexist. Some of these are also quite risky. On the contrary, there are others that can be considered less risky, and as such, reduce the overall risk of the investment.

19. Improve your Financial Intelligence

You are not born as a trader, but you can become one. Investors are not born like that, but they become one. How? This is done by studying and applying. In this case, brokers offer you the right solution to your problem: professional training courses and free video lessons, such as those offered by the IQ Option broker dedicated entirely to the financial markets and online trading.

Financial competence takes into consideration two very important aspects: competence and time. These are very important elements that can really change the cards on the table, and make a style of investment manageable and profitable that could become an anxiety-generating bloodbath for others.

Regarding the risk and its propensity to face it, the questions to be asked are two.

- The first is inherent in the time you have available to learn and, therefore, how much energy you are willing to devote to your investments.
- The second is how anxious you are about money and economic security. In this case, it is better to let go of this whole investing idea.

20. Buy stocks of a company without competitors

Even this advice may seem improper, but in reality, it is very effective.

For example, it is never advisable to invest in retail and automotive airlines. Generally, they are not considered good long-term investments.

In most cases, these are commercial sectors in which competition is very high. This means that if you look at their balance sheets, you can see how the profits are very low.

In general, do not invest in companies that generate a large part of their turnover in specific periods of the year, as are the airlines and those related to retail sales. Only in the case in which they have not shown profits and constant revenues, even in a long period of time, then it is convenient to do so.

21. Keep yourself updated about the news in the market

Always try to find all possible information before buying any shares. Choose only companies that have a certain solidity. Choose those that have a price momentarily lower than their real value. This concept is the essence behind the investments. You buy low and sell high.

We consider it as the keystone of being disciplined in carrying out the researches and the related market analyses and in evaluating the performance of investment by constantly checking it and making the necessary changes.

An example would be companies with an excellent brand which can be a good investment option. Coca-Cola, Johnson & Johnson, Procter & Gamble, 3M, and Exxon are all good examples.

22. Do not look at your portfolio every hour

This is because markets are volatile. You do not have to be influenced by the performance of world stock exchanges, because otherwise, you may even be tempted to liquidate your positions too early, losing an excellent long-term investment opportunity.

Before buying the shares of stock, you must also consider questions such as: "If the value of my shares were to go down, would I be more inclined to liquidate or buy more?" If you decide to liquidate them, do not buy any other shares.

23. Be aware of your prejudices and do not allow the emotions to influence your decisions

You must always believe in what you do and never get overwhelmed by emotion. Always believe in yourself and in the strategy behind your investments. Only by this, you will be on your way to becoming a successful investor.

All stock exchanges, like Wall Street, are focused on short-term investments. This is why it is difficult to predict possible future profits in case they are projected in the long-term.

In order to calculate the target of your investment (the price at which to sell your positions), make forecasts with a time horizon of more than 10 years and update them over time using the DCF.

24. Invest in those companies that hold shareholders in high esteem

In most cases, companies prefer to spend profits on buying a new personal jet for the CEO instead of paying dividends to shareholders.

A long-term management-oriented remuneration system, "stock-expensing," even if it is a prudent capital investment policy, a reliable dividend policy, a profit for growth stocks, and the BVPS ("Book-Value-Per-Share") are all indicators of a company oriented towards its shareholders.

25. Try out "paper trading"

In this case, it is a simulation of investments. In practice, this tool keeps track of the price of the shares and of all of your purchase and sale transactions, as if you were actually operating them on the market.

At the same time, you can check your investments if they have generated a profit or not.
Once you have identified a reliable and profitable strategy and you feel comfortable with the natural functioning of the market, you can move on to the real operational phase.

Finally, remember that you are not buying and selling worthless pieces of paper. The price rises and falls over time. You are buying shares in real companies.

Your decision to buy the shares of a particular company should be influenced only by two factors: the economic soundness of the company and the price of its shares.

26. Focus your thoughts

When analyzing the market, you should always try to formulate a plausible development scenario, and consequently, identify the good securities to invest in. We are sure that this passage serves you in order to make some forecasts in some specific areas.

An example would be the trend in interest rates and inflation, if not the way in which these variables can affect the yield of fixed-rate financial products or other assets. At the same time, when interest rates are low, it could be expected that consumers and businesses can access cash and credit more easily.

In practice, all this means that people have more money to use for their purchases and, therefore, tend to buy more. At the same time, companies, thanks to higher revenues, will be able to invest with the aim of expanding their activities. On the contrary, the opposite happens in the stock market; low-interest rates lead to an increase in the price of equities. At the same time, a high-interest rate generates a lowering of the value of the shares. At a time, when interest rates are high, investing becomes much more expensive. This means that you could try to invest in shares that offer a better return for you but that are not heavy for consumers.

An example could be a bank's shares. If you invest on the shares of a Bank X because the interest rates are high for you, you must also consider the interest rates that are applied to those who ask for a mortgage, for example. In this case, an interest rate for a high mute will soon make Bank X shares collapse because it is not convenient for the lender. Always evaluate all factors then.

In short, consumers spend less, companies have less liquidity for investments thus, there is a slowdown in economic growth or even a stalemate.

27. Create a wish list

In order to be able to establish your financial goals, you must always have a precise idea of the things or experiences you wish to possess. You can always choose only what you want to experience in life, and for which you need to earn money.

You must have a list of everything you want to get from this investment and then work out a lineup to guarantee your goals.

28. Diversify your portfolio

Investors with experience like Warren Buffett recommend diversifying their investments: a choice that serves to manage risks in a better way, as do the most prudent that focus on companies in different industries and in different countries, hoping that a bad event does not damage all their titles.

Imagine owning five different companies. At the end of the year, company A and B performed well and increased the value of the shares by 25%. C and D instead increased by 10%, while E had the worst lack and ended up in liquidation.

In this case, the diversification strategy helps you recover the losses of your total investment.

29. Understand the main financial instruments

Among the many solutions that are available to those who intend to invest, we want to talk about: Forex, binary options, ETFs, and commodities.

Proceeding by order, we clarify how Forex investments work. It is the largest market in the world today. Although it is simple to deposit and invest in the ratio of currencies, it is positively known that returns are so high as the same measure of losses. It is for this reason that experts are always advised to take advantage of the demos for general learning before proceeding with the use of real money. In any case, it is our advice to beginners to focus only on the performance of a currency pair, remembering to include the stop loss in the open position to avoid too large losses.

In regard to investments in binary options, these are available to anyone, as the previous solution, provided that some attention is always paid in these circumstances. This investment system concerns the launch of forecasts aimed at the performance of certain security over a given period of time. If the forecast is correct, there will be rather interesting profits. Even here, in order not to face unpleasant surprises, the same goes for the previous type of investment.

The ETF, those funds listed in real time that we mentioned, which go to replicate the index of a certain basket of securities, allow you to invest even with small amounts at lower costs than traditional funds. With these, you can trade on a wide variety of indices such as emerging markets, entire geographical areas, individual states, listed companies, etc. The advantages of investing using ETFs reside not only in their convenience, in being very liquid and tradable like equities, but also in the respective assets independent of the issuer.

30. Consider it a serious business

I truly believe that anyone can learn to trade options, currencies (Forex), commodities (Commodities), or cryptocurrencies. In the same way, I am convinced that with this system, you can become financially free. However, it must be approached as a serious business.

Let me ask you a question: how much did you study or work to achieve the experience you have in your current job? I imagine we are talking about several years and still thousands of hours of study and practice.

Trading is no different.

31. Be humble

When trading, you compete on a par with people who do it by profession: you must, therefore, have humility, work, perseverance, intelligence, and method. If you really apply, in a few months, you can decide to give up your job because you can earn a lot of money with something that requires commitment and constancy, but without being stressed or having to spend all day on the trading sites.

Conclusion

Thank you for making it through to the end of *Day Trading*. Let's hope it was informative and able to provide you with all of the tools you need to achieve your goals.

The next step is to find a broker you would like to use and get started with stocks. It is always a good idea to have a plan in place to help you to get started before just jumping in. Penny stocks are a bit harder compared to working with your traditional stock market, but it is a great way to make some money and see your portfolio grow.

Inside this guidebook, we took some time to discuss the stocks and how you would get started with them. We discussed how stocks are different from the traditional assets before moving on to some of the tips that you can follow in order to get into the market for stocks. Then, we spent a good deal of time talking about the different strategies that you can use when getting into stocks. The strategy is one of the most important steps to getting this started because it helps you to know what to look for when making your predictions and making money. We then ended with some great tips, as well as an overview of the SEC regulations on the stocks to help you fully understand what is going on with this industry.

When you are ready to get into investing or you are looking for a new way to expand out the portfolio and make some more money, stocks may be the answer that you are looking for. Make sure to look through this guidebook and learn as much as possible about working with stocks and how you can make money in this market.

Finally, if you found this book useful in any way, a review is always appreciated!

Description

Do not work for Money, let Money work for You
Discover the Hidden Secrets of Investing in the Stock Market

It is incredible how much wealth can be accumulated by investing in the stock market. However, it is even more fascinating to see that the average investors lose money in a year cycle. Why? Because the stock market is profitable only if you know the right strategies.

This book was born from the idea to create a crash course that could help a beginner avoid common mistakes and get the foot on the market without falling. It is not a secret that the best investors apply different techniques than those who are struggling. The aim of the book is to spread the right information and to give a proper overview of what works and what does not work when investing in the stock market.

During the course of this book, you will learn:

- What the stock market is and why it is a gold mine for those who know what to do
- A simplified dictionary with the most important terms
- 7 Standards a stock has to meet to represent a good opportunity (very important)
- The power of leverage and how it can help investors with a small capital
- The difference between Fundamental Analysis and Technical Analysis
- 10 Common mistakes made by beginners and how to avoid them
- The right way to diversify a portfolio and why it is important (not what you think)

As you can see, there is a lot to talk about. Do not worry, everything will be explained with simple terms and an easy to follow structure.

It is important to note that the book does not offer "get rich quick solutions". Easy money does not exist, especially at the early stages. However, by studying the material provided and applying it diligently, it is possible to successfully get started in a matter of weeks.

Are you ready to Kickstart your Investing Journey?